KU-298-430

Collins

FOOD *for* FREE

Collins

FOOD

for FREE

RICHARD MABEY

HarperCollins*Publishers*
77–85 Fulham Palace Road
London W6 8JB

The HarperCollins website address is:
www.**fire**and**water**.com

Collins is a registered trademark of HarperCollins*Publishers* Ltd.

07 06 05 04 03 02

10 9 8 7 6 5 4 3 2

ISBN 0 00 220159 3

© Richard Mabey 1972, 1989, 2001

The author asserts his moral right to be identified as the author of this
work. All rights reserved.

The copyright in the photographs belongs to Bob Gibbons, Natural Image
apart from the following.
Supplied by Natural Image: John Roberts: 60, 61, 114, 116, 117b, 151,
152cl, cr, 153bl, br, 154t, bl, 155br, 156bc, 158cl, bl, 158t, 161cl, bl, 162tl,
163cl, 169, 170, 173, 186, 187; Peter Wilson: 49t, 100, 172.
Alan Outen: 162bl, 163tl, bl.
Supplied by Premaphotos Wildlife: Ken Preston-Mafham 55tr, Dr Rod
Preston-Mafham 53, 57.

Designed by Colin Brown

Colour reproduction by Colourscan, Singapore

Printed and bound by Proost, Belgium

Contents

Introduction

Today our supermarkets offer us an ever-wider and even bewildering selection of fruit and vegetables from all over the world. We can buy strawberries all year around, and more exotic foods are no longer prohibitively expensive. However, with the development of genetically-modified foods, fears over irradiation, and mass-farming causing worries over health issues, there has been something of a backlash. Now Michelin-starred chefs are advocating the joys of rock samphire, a native coastal plant that goes beautifully with another national, but nonetheless endangered food, fish.

My reaction the first time I was offered a plate of wild vegetables was fear. I regarded the dish, of what looked like shiny, green pipecleaners, with trepidation: what was it? Was it poisonous? Would it be worth tasting? When I finally lifted the forkful of what turned out to be marsh samphire, all my worries were dispelled.

To some extent, we have become conditioned by the shrink-wrapped, perfectly-shaped, 'hero' produce we find in our supermarkets, and it is the irregularity, and the feeling that eating foods we pick ourselves in uncultivated areas is somehow unhygienic, that makes us reluctant to venture into woods, pastures, clifftops and marshlands in search of food. In fact almost every British garden vegetable (not including greenhouse species), has a wild ancestor flourishing here: wild parsnips, cabbage and celery all grow in waste places. Historically these have always been sources of food in times of hardship, but we seem to know less and less about them, and are becoming less confident about identifying them.

This is a practical guide to these plants, both a manual and a history of how they have been, and still can be used today. I can't pretend that it is possible to exist entirely on the wild foods you can find in the woods and fields at the end of your garden, indeed, many people have no wild places close at hand. Even if you could find a plentiful supply, collecting your daily groceries could become a full-time job! Wild plants may not even be any more nutritious than their supermarket counterparts, but they are likely to be relatively free from herbicides and other agricultural treatments.

The busy lifestyles of today automatically preclude such activities, but I would offer the following incentives. My attraction to wild foods is somewhat self-indulgent: I enjoy the whole ritual associated with locating, smelling, identifying and collecting the plants, and the sense of achievement that goes with it. I also relish the different textures and flavours of these foods, and this I think, is what will astonish most people. It brings a realisation of just to what extent the cultivation and mass production of food have muted our taste experiences. The second is that finding out about the history of our native plants is a fascinating pastime; the stories, anecdotes and local legends are all as much a part of our national heritage as our local flora and fauna, and we should make the effort to keep all these alive. Finally, many of our wild foods are delicacies – delicious and highly-prized – and they are all free. The joy of discovery is an exhilarating experience and our hunter-gatherer instincts are encouraged to come to the fore.

In more recent times, most use has been made of wild foods in remote areas, in times of economic hardship or when harvests were poor. I trust that situations like this, in this country at least, are unlikely to arise again. But does this mean that the only reasons we have to collect and cook wild foods is through idle curiosity or the thrill of the chase? Our native flora is in fact a museum of the past; to know their history is to understand how intricately food is bound up with the whole pattern of our social lives. It is easy to forget this when our food is instantly and effortlessly available, and working on the land seems a relic from a bygone era. We take our food for granted as we do our air and water, and all three can be threatened as a result.

Yet understanding the biology of just a few of the plants in this book does give an insight into the complex and delicate relationship which plants have with their environment; their dependence on birds to carry their seeds, livestock to eat the grass that shuts out the light, thereby allowing them to grow, and the wind, sunshine and the balance of chemicals in the soil which means they can be harvested.

There are those who would not welcome a new generation going out and harvesting our wild foods. However, informing people about the environment, and becoming part of it is the best way to encourage a continuation of this delicate balance. One of the most complex and intimate relationships which most of us can have with our environment is to eat it. I would hope that this book will not encourage rural vandalism, but will deepen respect for the landscape and for the interdependence of living things.

This book covers the majority of wild plant food products that can be obtained in the British Isles, but there are some categories that have been deliberately omitted. There is nothing on grasses and cereals. This is intended as a practical guide, and no-one is going to spend time hand-gathering enough seeds to grind into flour. I have briefly touched on the traditional herbal uses of many plants where this is interesting or relevant. But I have included no plants purely on the grounds of their presumed therapeutic value.

The book has been organised by season. Many plants only bear flowers or fruits in one particular season and the species accounts have therefore been placed within the relevant season. Where a plant contains parts that appear in different seasons, then the species account appears in the season that produces the food of most value. Some foods are available all year round, even in winter, and that is where it will be described. Please refer to the index for any plants you would like to locate within the text.

How to Use Wild Foods

Roots

Roots are probably the least practical of all wild vegetables. First, few species produce large, fleshy roots in the wild, and the coarse wiry roots of species such as wild parsnip and horseradish, mean they are only really suitable for flavouring. Second, it is against the law to dig up wild plants by the root except on your own land, or with permission of the landowner.

Green vegetables

The main problem with wild leaf vegetables is their size. Not many wild plants have the big, floppy leaves for which cultivated greens have been bred, and as a result, picking enough for a serving can be a tiresome one. For this reason the optimum picking time for most leaf vegetables is probably their middle age, when the flowers are out and the plant is easy to recognise, and the leaves have reached maximum size without beginning to wither. Green vegetables can be divided into salads, cooked greens and stems; see dandelion for salads, sea beet or fat hen for greens, and alexanders for stems.

All green vegetables can also be made into soup, sauces or cooked medleys or 'messes' of different types of green leaves.

Herbs

Herbs are leafy, green plants that are used as flavourings for other foods. Most wild herbs in fact have a milder flavour than their domestic counterparts; being valued principally for their flavouring qualities, it is these which domestication has attempted to intensify, not delicacy, size, succulence or any of the other qualities that are sought after in staple vegetables.

The best time to pick a herb, especially for the purposes of drying, is just as it is coming into flower. This is the stage at which the plant's nutrients and aromatic oils are still mainly concentrated in the leaves, yet it will have a few blossoms to assist with the identification. Gather your herbs in dry weather and preferable early in the morning before they have been exposed to too much sun. Wet herbs will tend to develop mildew during drying, and specimens picked after long exposure to strong sunshine will inevitably have lost some of their natural oils by evaporation.

Cut whole stalks of the herb with a knife to avoid damaging the parent plant. If you are going to use the herbs fresh, strip the leaves and flowers off the stalks as soon as you get them home. If you are going to dry them, leave the stalks intact as you have picked them. To maintain their colour and flavour they must be dried as quickly as possible, but without too intense a heat. Therefore they need a combination of gentle warmth and good ventilation, such as an airing cupboard, or a kitchen. Hang the stalks in bunches (it is a good idea to warp them in muslin to keep out the flies, and to catch any loose leaves as they crumble and fall), or arrange on a sheet of paper and place on a shelf above the stove. All herbs can be used to flavour vinegar, oils or drinks.

Spices

The seeds of aromatic plants can also be used as flavourings, although they cannot necessarily be used as direct substitutes for the leaves, as there are subtle differences in flavour. The seeds should be left to dry on the plant, and when they are dry and ready to drop off the plant then this is the point at which their food content and flavour should be at its maximum.

Flowers

Gathering wild flowers for no other reason than their diverting flavours would be anti-social, and in the case of some rare species, it is also illegal. Some of the flowers mentioned in the book are rare, and these have been included for historical reasons only. The only species I advocate picking from, and in small quantities, are the common, hardy perennial plants that do not rely on seeding for continued survival. They are mostly bushes or shrubs in which each individual produces an abundant number of blossoms.

Fruits

Some fruits included in this book are cultivated and sold commercially as well as growing in the wild. Where this is the case I have not concentrated on common kitchen uses, but instead I have given more space to details of how to find and gather the wild berries, and on more unusual and traditional recipes.

Jellies and jams can be made from most soft fruits, although the amount of pectin needed to help the jams to set varies from fruit to fruit (see p.138). The first stage is to pulp the fruits: cover with just enough water and simmer until mushy. Depending on the hardness of the skin this may take up to half an hour and require help with the back of a spoon. Then separate the juice from the pulp by straining through muslin; let the muslin bag hang so that the juice drips into a bowl (you can also use a stocking). To gain the maximum amount of juice leave this to strain overnight.

When you have the juice you want, measure it and transfer to a clean pan, adding 500g (1lb) of sugar for each 500ml (1 pint) of juice. Bring to the boil stirring well and boil rapidly. Skim off any scum that floats to the surface. A jelly will normally form when the mixture has reached a temperature of 105°C (221°F). If you do not have a jam thermometer then you can test the mixture by putting a drop onto a cold saucer. If setting is imminent the drop will not run after a few seconds as a skin will have formed across it. As soon as this state has been achieved, transfer the mixture into clean, warm jars, and cover the surface with a wax disk and then a cellophane cover, pulled taut and sealed with a rubber band. Label and store in a cool place.

Fruit can also be stewed, dried or used to flavour wines and liqueurs.

Nuts

Nuts are the major source of second-class protein and can be used in meals to form the main protein content of a meal. However, wild nuts are also extremely important to the survival of many wild birds and animals, and should not be picked to excess. If you do wish to try wild nuts pick and store them dry as they can rot. Use them in salads or with vegetable dishes.

SPRING

When daisies pied and violets blue,

And lady-smocks all silver-white,

And cuckoo-buds of yellow hue

Do paint the meadows with delight.

SPRING AND WINTER, William Shakespeare 1564–1616

DESCRIPTION
Shrub up to 8m (26ft)
high.

LEAVES
glossy green and deeply
lobed on spiny branches.

FLOWERS
abundant umbels of
white (sometimes pink),
strongly scented
blossoms, April–June.

HABITAT
woods, hedges,
scrubland, and on heaths
and downs. Common
throughout Europe.

Hawthorn
Crataegus monogyna

The young leaves of the hawthorn are probably the first wild vegetable a country child eats, and in England they are widely known as 'bread and cheese'. This hasn't anything to do with the taste of the leaves, and is probably a metaphor for their character as a very basic foodstuff. (Some hardy children eat the older leaves, the bread, together with the young red berries, like Dutch cheeses, in late summer.)

Whatever the origins of their name, the young leaves, picked between April and May, have a pleasantly nutty taste, and make a good addition to real bread and cheese sandwiches. More formally, try them chopped in a cold potato salad, or, for a spectacular colour contrast, with diced beetroot.

A sauce for spring lamb can be made by chopping the leaves with other early wild greens, such as garlic mustard and sorrel, and dressing with vinegar and brown sugar, as with a mint sauce.

Dorothy Hartley gives a splendid recipe for a hawthorn spring pudding, for those with the patience to collect large numbers of the unopened leaf buds. Make a light suet crust, well-seasoned, and roll it out thinly and as long in shape as possible. Cover the surface with the young buds and push them lightly into the dough. Take some rashers of bacon, cut into fine strips

and lay them across the leaves. Moisten the edges of the dough and roll it up tightly, sealing the edges as you go. Tie in a pudding cloth and steam for at least an hour. Cut it in thick slices, like a Swiss roll, and serve with plenty of gravy.

A final trick with hawthorn twigs, very appropriate for foragers: take a well-branched twig about 30cm (12in) tall, strip it of leaves, and place in a pot. Use it to dry mushrooms by impaling their caps on the spines, and placing the whole potful close to a fire or radiator.

DESCRIPTION
A tall climber 3–6m
(10–20ft).

LEAVES
toothed, five-lobed.

FLOWERS
male, small and green in
panicles, female in
rounded clusters,
July–August.

FRUITS
cone-like, September.

HABITAT
widely scattered in
hedgerows, woodland
edges, scrub and
wasteland, throughout
Europe.

Hop
Humulus lupulus

Hop is a familiar perennial climber, especially in the southern half of England, and notorious for ascending telephone poles as well as tall hedges. It is a native plant, though in hop-growing areas some specimens may be escapes from cultivation. Hops are best known for the role of their cone-like fruits in the brewing of beer, first started in Holland and Germany, and later incorporateded into British brewing practises.

Its other role in the kitchen also has connection with the brewing business. During the pruning of the cultivated hopvines in May (often done by gangs of volunteer labour, as was the picking of the hops the pruned shoots, up to about 15cm (6in) long, were tied in bundles and cooked as asparagus. Pliny mentions the very same practice 2,000 years before.

In the Mediterranean hop shoots are one of the very many spring vegetables that are cooked with eggs. In Italy they are used in a kind of omelette (see right).

Hop frittata

Frittata is an Italian recipe that can be used with many of the green stem wild vegetables in this book, for example, wild asparagus, wild garlic, thistles and bramble shoots. A frittata should be much more solid than an omelette and can be served hot or cold.

Two handfuls of hop shoots

1 small onion

4 eggs

1 dessertspoon of dried breadcrumbs

1 dessertspoon of parmesan cheese

parsley

1 Beat the eggs with seasoning to taste, and with the breadcrumbs and parmesan cheese.

2 Chop the hop tops into roughly 5cm (2in) lengths and fry with the chopped onion in a little olive oil in a heavy pan until they have both begun to brown.

3 Add the beaten egg mixture, and simmer over a low heat. In about four or five minutes the frittata should have set.

4 Take a large plate, cover the pan and turn over so that the frittata settles onto it. Then slide it back into the pan, and simmer until the other side is brown.

Sweet Gale, Bog Myrtle
Myrica gale

DESCRIPTION

A deciduous shrub 0.5–2m (1½–6½ft) high.

FLOWERS

red and orange (male and female) catkins on separate plants, flowers appear in April or May before the leaves.

LEAVES

grey-green, narrow and toothed, on shiny reddish twigs.

DISTRIBUTION

locally common, mainly in northern parts of Britain and Europe.

HABITAT

bogs, marshes and wet heaths.

Before the extensive draining of fen and wet wasteland that began in the 16th Century, sweet gale must have been a much more widespread plant. Now it is only locally common in wet, acid heathland and moors, mainly in north Wales, the north-west of England and Scotland. Some small, local populations do occur in southern England and the Norfolk Broads. But where it does appear, its leaves and flowers can scent the whole area with their delightfully sweet, resinous smell.

Gale was traditionally used for the flavouring of beer before hops became the customary agent in this country. There is evidence that this drink was being brewed in Anglo-Saxon times, and the isolated patches which grow around old monasteries and other early settlements suggest that it was occasionally taken into cultivation beyond its usual habitats. Its warm aroma – with hints of balsam, cloves and pine resin – will also give a retsina-like tang to wine, if sprigs of bog myrtle are steeped in the wine (in re-sealed bottles) for a month.

ABOVE
Bog myrtle on Hartland
Moor, Dorset.

The obsolete local name of 'candle berries' refers to the old practice of extracting a vegetable wax from shoots of the plant. The wax is carried in tiny yellow glands along the young twigs, leaves and fruit, and was extracted by boiling the shoots in salted water. The wax floats to the surface like a scum, was skimmed off and used to make small candles – though large quantities of myrtle needed to be gathered.

The same process is still carried out, rather more effectively, with the exceptionally waxy north American shrub, the bayberry or wax myrtle, *Myrica cerifera*. It grows in thickets near swamps and marshes in the sand-belt near the Atlantic coast and on the shore of Lake Erie. The globular berries produce wax which was traditionally removed by boiling them in water and skimming the wax off the top. Candles made from this plant's wax are grey-green in colour and burn with a mildly spicy fragrance. They are smokeless after snuffing and very brittle. They are sold in Cape Cod tourist shops, an ironic reminder of a time when they were a vital source of light, not just a table decoration. They were also used as sealing wax.

DESCRIPTION
A coarse, upright
perennial, covered with
fine, stinging hairs.

LEAVES
toothed and heart
shaped.

FLOWERS
thin catkins of
undistinguished green
flowers, June–September.

DISTRIBUTION
widespread and often
abundant throughout
Europe.

HABITAT
waste and cultivated
ground, wet woods,
hedgebanks, river valley.

Stinging Nettle
Urtica doica

Be warned: to be caught eating nettles will cause more consternation amongst your friends than the munching of any number of other more dubious plants. They will never quite believe that the chemicals responsible for the sting are not utterly destroyed by cooking.

Yet the stinging nettle is probably the most widespread and prolific of all edible wildings, and one of the most useful. The Romans used the stems as a warming scourge against rheumatism. Nettles were cultivated in 18th-Century Scandinavia, the coarse fibres of the stalks being used for cloth as well as the leaves for food. Samuel Pepys enjoyed a nettle porridge on 25 February 1661, though he gives no details of the dish. Sir Walter Scott had the old gardener in *Rob Roy* raising nettles under glass as 'early spring kail'. And in the Second World War hundreds of tons were gathered annually in Britain for the extraction of chlorophyll, and to be used as dye for camouflage nets.

Nettles and people are plainly old companions. And wherever the soil has been enriched by the refuse of human settlement – be it in boneyards or back gardens – there will be nettles. Because they take up nutrients very slowly, nettles can be astonishingly persistent on such sites. In woods in the Salisbury area they are still flourishing on the buried refuse of Romano-British villages abandoned 1,600 years ago.

The striking ability of nettles to make use of minerals and nitrogen in enriched soils gives them a high ranking in nourishment tables. They have high levels of Vitamins A and C, 2.3 per cent by weight of iron, and a remarkable 5.5 per cent of protein.

Young leaves should be picked between late February and early June, using scissors and gloves for comfort. Gather only the youngest leaves from the top of each plant. Older leaves – especially those formed after June – contain tiny crystalline particles which make the texture gritty. They are also bitter and can often have a laxative effect. The very best nettles are the whole shoots picked when they are just a few centimeteres high in March.

A basic recipe, and the first step in some more elaborate dishes, is a nettle puree. Strip the leaves from the coarser stalks, wash, and place in pan with no more water than adheres to the leaves. Simmer for four or five minutes, then strain well, add a large knob of butter and plenty of seasoning (and perhaps some chopped onion) and simmer for a further five, turning and mashing all the while. The resulting puree is interestingly fluffy in texture, but don't expect it to taste like spinach, as is sometimes suggested. Nettle puree has a mild taste all its own, a little like pea-pods if one has to find a comparison. Use it as a vegetable on its own, spread it on toast and serve with a poached egg on top, or mix into balls with oatmeal and fry in bacon fat as a kind of rissole. A variation on this last is a 6th-Century Irish recipe for 'St Columba's broth', in which the puree is warmed in a mixture of milk and water, to which fine oatmeal is slowly stirred in until the mixture thickens.

More modern recipes include deep-frying the leaves to the consistency of green crisps, and Anton Mossiman's pâté, made by blending cooked nettles, new potatoes and fromage blanc. Young nettle leaves have also been made into beer and used for a herbal tea.

Nettle soup

4 large handfuls of nettle tops

I large onion

50g (2oz) butter

2 potatoes

II (2 pints) of vegetable stock

I tablespoon of crème fraiche

Seasoning, including grated nutmeg

I Strip the nettles from the thicker stalks, and wash.

2 Melt the butter and simmer the chopped onion until golden

3 Add the nettles (or an equivalent amount of nettle puree – see above), and the chopped potatoes, and cook for two to three minutes.

4 Add the stock, and simmer for 20 minutes, using a wooden spoon from time to time to crush the potatoes.

5 Add the seasoning, plus a little grated nutmeg, and serve with a swirl of crème fraiche.

6 Or, if you would prefer a smoother soup, put the mixture through a liquidizer first. Reheat, and add seasoning and crème fraiche.

DESCRIPTION
A clump or patch-
forming perennial.

FLOWERS
pink spikes topping a
straight hairless stem, up
to 70cm (28in),
June–September.

LEAVES
oblong or arrow-shaped
on long, winged stalks,
and showing silvery hairs
on the veins beneath.

HABITAT
damp grassland and
mountainous, areas and
on roadsides and stream
banks. Found in most of
Europe, except the far
north.

Bistort

Polygonum bistorta

In parts of northern England there is a tradition of making Easter puddings – 'Dock puddings' – from bistort leaves, and various combinations of oatmeal, egg and other green herbs. This is probably a local version of the custom still widespread in rural areas of Europe and America of eating bitter herbs at the beginning of spring, supposedly to cleanse the system of fats accumulated during winter and of the 'dull humours' produced by Lenten fasting. Why bistort should have been singled out as the vital ingredient in the sheep-grazing country of the north Pennines is hard to say. It certainly can be locally plentiful in damp hill pastures, and the leaves can be quite fleshy by Easter. But just as important may be the fact that bistort leaves have a comparatively mild taste, unlike some of the other customary ingredients of spring puddings. Many of the plant's local names reflect its function in this pudding, from Passion Dock (from Passion-Tide, the last two weeks of Lent) to Easter Ledge or Ledger, and Easter Giant, the last being a contraction of Easter Mangiant (from the French 'manger' meaning 'to eat').

Like many local customs, the making of Dock or Ledger puddings has declined this century. But in the late 1960s and early 1970s there was a revival, and in the spring of 1971 the following advertisement appeared in the personal columns of the Times. '*Polygonum bistorta* – How is your Dock Pudding?'. The notice invited entrants for the first World Championship Dock Pudding Contest, to be held in the Calder Valley in Yorkshire, around the villages of Hebden Bridge and Mytholmroyd. Evidently the tradition was far from dead here and there were over 50 entrants from this one valley alone.

The competition is still kept up and the competitors are required to follow a basic recipe including bistort leaves, chopped nettles, onions, and oatmeal, all fried in bacon fat. But dock pudding is a dish for which every village, and maybe every family, has its own recipe. The widest variety are in Cumbria, south and east of Carlisle, where there is even a kind of bistort leaf kebab, involving the skewering of the leaves and their subsequent simmering in milk and butter.

Dock pudding or rissoles

This is based on a recipe from Carlisle.

1 handful of bistort leaves
1 tablespoon each of the leaves of
nettles, cabbage or young leaves and
shoots from Brussels sprouts, and
dandelion or common dock
3 leeks
2 blackcurrant leaves
1 cup of cooked pearl barley
3 eggs
Oatmeal for binding and/or coating
Salt and pepper to taste
Oil or bacon fat

1 Chop the bistort, leeks and other greens roughly and blanch in water for a few minutes.

2 Mix with the pearl barley, seasoning and two of the eggs, hard-boiled and chopped, and the other egg beaten, season and then bind with a little oatmeal.

3 There are two alternatives ways to cook the rissoles. Either put in a pudding basin and boil for ten minutes, or, form the mixture into balls, coat in oatmeal, and fry in oil or bacon fat.

DESCRIPTION
Erect perennial
10–120cm(4–47in) high.

LEAVES
arrow-shaped and
clasping the stem near
the top of the plant.

FLOWERS
spikes of small red and
green flowers on a
smooth stem,
May–August.

HABITAT
grassy places, meadows,
pastures, roadsides and
heaths. Widespread
throughout Europe.

Sorrel

Rumex acetosa

An indication of the rather special taste of sorrel leaves lies in the fact that they were once used as fillings for tarts and turnovers in Lancashire in the months between the last apples in March and the first gooseberries. They have a decidedly fruity taste, like plum skins when raw and rhubarb (a member of the same botanical family) when cooked.

Sorrel is one of the first green plants to appear in spring. The shield- or arrow-shaped leaves can often be picked in March, when other greenstuff is scarce. Look for them in the shadier corners of damp grassland, as the leaves tend to grown larger there. They are marvellously cool and sharp when raw, but perhaps too acid for some palates – though John Clare has his parched fieldworkers in *The Shepherd's Calendar* chewing them neat:

> '*The mower gladly chews it down*
> *And slakes his thirst the best he may.*'

They make a good lemony addition to salads throughout the spring and summer, especially if you cut or tear the strips across the grain (what the French refer to as chiffonade). You may need to pull the rib from some of the larger leaves.

In Gerard's time the leaves were boiled and eaten, or made into a green sauce for fish. For this they were pulped raw and mixed with sugar and vinegar. Dorothy Hartley describes a late 17th Century recipe for the sauce, in which bread, apple, sugar and vinegar are boiled together until soft, then mixed still hot, with sorrel puree. The mixture is strained, giving a thick green juice with a strong, pungent taste.

A common fault with sorrel, especially in early recipes, is to overcook the leaves until they have become a khaki-coloured sludge. They properly need a few seconds – minutes at the most – until the leaves have just wilted, and changed colour from emerald green to green-brown.

On the continent, where sorrel is used much more than in Britain, they are more respectful. A classic French dish is sorrel omelette, for which the secret is to add sliced strips of sorrel leaves just before the eggs set. They should change colour and wilt just as the omelette is ready. In France the leaves are added to give a sharp contrast to heavy dishes of potato, lentil and haricot bean, and to rich, fatty foods like pork, oily fish and avocado.

From further south comes a recipe for sorrel gazpacho. Put trimmed sorrel leaves into a blender with chicken stock and slices of stale white bread with the crusts removed. Blend until smooth. Add a little crème fraiche if desired, blend again and chill. Then serve garnished with croutons, prawns or chopped hard-boiled egg.

Sorrel can also be used as a puree (boiled briefly, strained well then beaten with a fork or in a blender) – either as a vegetable in its own right, or as a green sauce (blended with olive oil and seasoning), or as a filling for a 'fruit' tart.

Sorrel soup

Two handfuls of sorrel

1 knob of butter

1 tbsp olive oil

1 onion

2 large potatoes

Salt and pepper to taste

1 tbsp yoghurt or crème fraiche

1 Wash and roughly chop two good handfuls of sorrel.

2 In a deep pan put a good knob of butter and a little olive oil, and sweat the onion, finely chopped, until softened.

3 Add the diced potatoes, and the seasoning, and cover with water.

4 Boil rapidly until the potatoes break up.

5 Then add the sorrel and simmer for a further two minutes, stirring all the while.

6 Serve, stirring in yoghurt or crème fraiche if you prefer a richer soups.

Good King Henry
Chenopodium bonus-henricus

DESCRIPTION
Medium perennial, often
reddish.

LEAVES
triangular, spear-shaped,
almost untoothed.

FLOWERS
in spikes, May–August.

HABITAT
by roadsides and in
cultivated ground.
Widespread but local;
less common in Wales,
Scotland, Ireland and the
South-west

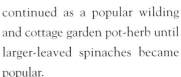

Good King Henry's curious name has nothing to do with Henry VIII or any other king. It is a corruption of 'Good Henry', an elfin figure from Saxon folklore whose name was applied to the plant to distinguish it from 'Bad Henry', the poisonous annual mercury (*Mercurialis annua*) with which it sometimes grows but in no way resembles.

Good King Henry is a native of the Mediterranean, and its seeds may have been brought over as weeds by the first farmers over 5,000 years ago, and taken advantage of disturbed or cultivated ground. Since plants tend to grow larger and more successfully on rich and fertilised soils they would have been naturally commoner in the well-manured waste places – muck heaps, animal pens, muddy waysides (still their habitats today – immediately suggesting themselves as candidates for cultivation. They continued as a popular wilding and cottage garden pot-herb until larger-leaved spinaches became popular.

Good King Henry is a perennial, which means leaves can be picked from it continuously, as from an everlasting spinach. It has lately come back into popularity (and commerce) as a herb-garden species.

The leaves can be cooked as a spinach, and the stems as an inferior asparagus. A recipe from England's Fens involves cutting the young shoots when they are no more than 20cm (8in) high, stripping off the larger leaves, binding in small bundles, and then simmering in water for no more than eight minutes serve with melted butter.

Sea Beet, Sea Spinach

Beta vulgaris ssp. *maritima*

DESCRIPTION
A perennial up to 1m
(3ft) tall.

LEAVES
shiny, fleshy, available
most of the year.

FLOWERS
tiny green blooms in long
leafy spikes,
June–September.

HABITAT
common around the
coastline, on cliffs,
shingle banks, dunes,
sea-walls. Found in much
of Europe.

One of the happy exceptions to the small-leaved tendency among wild vegetables. Some of the lower leaves of sea beet can grow as large and as heavy as those of its cousin spinach, and creak like parchment when you touch them.

The wild plant is one of the ancestors of our cultivated beets, from mangolds through to chards and spinach-beet. Cultivation was begun at least 2,000 years ago in the Middle East and was mostly directed towards filling out the long tap root into the forms we now pickle, feed to cattle or convert to sugar. If you look closely at some of the wild specimens you will

occasionally find a red-veined individual that is from the strain that was developed into the beetroot.

The leaves have been changed little by cultivation, except to lose some of their powerful tannin-and-iron flavour. You can pick them between April and November – big, fleshy ones from the base of the plant and thinner, spear-shaped ones near the head. Try and strip the larger leaves from the spine as you pick them: it will save time during the preparation for cooking.

Always take special care in washing wild spinach leaves (especially if they have been picked near public footpaths), and remove the stray herbage you will have inevitably gathered up whilst picking the leaves, together with the more substantial stalks.

Sea beet can be used in similar ways to its relative garden spinach, *Spinacia oleracea*. Small leaves which grow on specimens very close to the sea are both tender and succulent (up to 1mm thick sometimes) and are ideal for salads. Larger ones should be steamed, or boiled briskly in a large saucepan with no more than 1cm (½in) of water at the bottom. Leave the lid on for a few minutes, and at intervals chop and press down the leaves. When they have all changed colour to a dark green the beet is cooked. Remove the lid and simmer for two or three minutes to boil off some of the remaining water, then transfer to a colander and press out as much liquid as possible, saving it if you wish for stocks and gravies. Return the greens to the saucepan and toss very briefly with a knob of butter. Some good additions to sea beet cooked in this way are diced tomatoes and chopped hazel nuts.

An intriguing recipe for sea beet is a 17th-Century spinach tart. Chop up the cooked leaves with a couple of hard-boiled egg yolks. Set into a pastry tart case, and pour on a sauce made of melted sugar, raisins and a touch of cinnamon. Bake in a moderate oven for half an hour.

Mussels with sea beet

The maritime savour of sea beet makes it a natural companion for fresh mussels. Hugh Fearnley-Whittingstall combines the two directly with a béchamel sauce.

500g (1lb) sea beet

250 ml (½ pint) milk

75g (3oz) butter

50g (2oz) flour

50g (2oz) breadcrumbs

Nutmeg

2 tbsp Parmesan cheese grated

2 crushed cloves of garlic

1 glass of white wine

1kg (2lb) fresh mussels, scrubbed and de-bearded

1 Cook the sea beet as above, squeeze as dry as possible and chop finely.

2 Warm the milk but do not boil. In another pan melt 50g (2oz) of the butter and slowly blend in the flour. Stir to remove any lumps and cook for a few minutes. Add the milk slowly, stirring all the time until the béchamel sauce thickens. Then stir in the chopped sea beet, half the grated Parmesan and a pinch of nutmeg.

3 In another pan melt a knob of butter and fry the crushed garlic cloves for a minute. Add the wine and a little water. When this mixture is boiling rapidly add the mussels, and steam until they are all open (discarding any that fail to open).

4 Remove all the mussel meat from the shells, and stir into the sea beet mixture. Thin with a little of the liquor (strained) produced from cooking the mussels. Season if necessary.

5 Spread the mixture into an ovenproof dish. Mix the breadcrumbs with the rest of the Parmesan and sprinkle over the top.

6 Bake for ten minutes in a preheated oven at Gas Mark 6/200°C/400°F.

Chickweed

Stellaria media

DESCRIPTION
A weak annual which tends to straggle and creep before it has reached any height. It has lines of fine hairs down the stem.

LEAVES
oval, bright green and soft.

FLOWERS
throughout the year, tiny white star-like flowers with five deeply divided petals.

HABITAT
gardens, cultivated and waste ground. Widespread and common throughout Europe.

The pale, soft green leaves of chickweed can be picked in almost any month of the year, except when there has been a hard frost. In fact they are often at their freshest in late autumn or early in the new year. They are one of the tenderest of wild greens, with a taste reminiscent of corn salad or a mild lettuce. John Gerard prescribed them for:

'little birdes in cadges … when they loath their meat'.

Even in his time chickweed was cooked as a green vegetable, and hawked around city streets by itinerant vegetable sellers.

You may find chickweed as a garden weed, or at the edges of arable fields. But avoid areas that may have been sprayed with weedkiller. The

leaves are too small to be picked individually, so strip bunches of the whole plant; the stems are just as tender as the leaves. Or choose the younger, greener sprigs more discriminately and cut with scissors.

The texture and mild taste of chickweed is probably best appreciated in a salad. Try mixing with hairy bittercress, wintercress and cow parsley, and dress with a mixture of lemon juice, a light vegetable oil (such as sunflower), a little sugar and seasoning. Or, cook alone for no more than two minutes, any longer and both taste and texture will go and the chickweed begin to resemble strands of green string. Wash and put into a saucepan without any additional water. Add a knob of butter, seasoning, some chopped spring onion, and simmer briefly. Finish off with a dash of lemon juice or a sprinkle of nutmeg.

Spring Greens

The young shoots and leaves of a large numbers of other wayside plants can be added to 'messes of greens'. In spring, to a base comprising a combination of chickweed, dandelion, fat-hen and stinging nettle add:

1. Very young dock leaves (*Rumex* species) for a slight bitter touch; bladder campion shoots (*Silene vulgaris*) ox-eye daisy leaf crowns (*Leucanthemum vulgaris*), white and red dead-nettles (*Lamium* species) and oraches (*Chenopodium* and *Atriplex* species), all for body.

2. Shepherd's purse (*Capsella bursa-pastoris*), lady's smock (*Cardamine pratensis*), common penny-cress (*Thlaspi arvense*), white mustard (of 'mustard and cress', *Sinapis alba*), and hairy bittercress (*Cardamine hirsuta*) for bite and pepperiness.

3. Blanched rosebay willowherb shoots (*Chaemerion angustifolium*) for a slightly fruity addition.

4. Many other leaves and flowers described in this book can also be added to provide taste, texture and colour.

DESCRIPTION
Annual
5–25cm(2–10in).

LEAVES
compound, cress-like.

FLOWERS
white, small, in
branched clusters,
February–September.

HABITAT
gardens and waste
ground, paths, walls; also
rocks and sand-dunes.
Found throughout
Europe.

BELOW
Cuckooflower,
Cardamine pratensis

Hairy Bittercress
Cardamine hirsuta

Hairy bittercress is one of the first edible weeds to be pickable early in the year. It is an annual of gardens and disturbed ground throughout Europe, with typical cress-like compound leaves, and small white flowers between February and September. The whole plant can be eaten, and has a pleasantly sweet, mild peppery flavour. It can be used in salads, sandwiches, as a substitute for cress, and has an affinity with cream cheese.

The slightly more spicy leaves of lady's smock, or cuckooflower (*Cardamine pratensis*), can be used in the same way. A medium, hairless perennial, cuckooflower is a common and widespread species of roadsides, river banks, ditches and damp grassland. The name 'cuckooflower' is shared at a local level with a number of other spring flowers, as they were an indicator of when the cuckoo was first heard in the year. However, for *Cardamine pratensis*, the belief that the first flowering of the plant heralds the spring song of the cuckoo, has been proven in a number of areas throughout the country, from Farnham in Surrey, to Dumfries in Scotland.

Jack-by-the-hedge, Hedge Garlic

Alliaria petiolata

DESCRIPTION
Annual or biennial, up
to 70cm (28in) tall.

LEAVES
a fresh green and slightly
toothed.

FLOWERS
small and brilliant white,
April–June.

HABITAT
waysides, on hedgebanks
and in open woods.
Widespread and common
throughout Europe.

Welcome previews of the spring, the soft leaves of hedge garlic can sometimes be seen as early as February if there has been a mild winter. If a warm autumn follows there is often a second crop of stubby, flowerless shoots in September and October.

For those who like garlic, but only in moderation, jack-by-the-hedge is ideal as a flavouring. When bruised or chopped the leaves give off just a suspicion of the smell of its unrelated namesake. Yet one Dr Prior, in *Popular Names of British Plants*, clearly thought otherwise when he gave this bizarre explanation for the common name of the plant:

'Jack or Jakes, latrina, alluding to its offensive smell.'

Jack-by-the-hedge is a pleasant plant, upright, balanced in colouring and classically simple in construction, and only a few leaves should be picked from each specimen. Some of the local names show that the kitchen use of the leaves has a long history. Turner mentions it, and Charles Bryant in his exhaustive *Flora Diaetetica* explain how it was used in the mid-18th Century:

'The poor people in the country eat the leaves of this plant with their bread, and on account of the relish they give, call them Sauce-alone. They also mix them with Lettuce, use them as a stuffing herb to pork, and eat them with salt-fish.'

Today it is still useful finely chopped in salads, but best possibly as a sauce for lamb. In the early spring, chop the leaves with hawthorn buds and a little mint, mix well with vinegar and sugar just as you would a pure mint sauce, and serve with the lamb.

Wood Sorrel

Oxalis acetosella

DESCRIPTION
Low, creeping plant.

LEAVES
shamrock-shaped and
lime-green when young.
5–15cm (2–6in) high.

FLOWERS
five white petals on a
delicate stem,
April–May.

HABITAT
woods and shady places
throughout Europe.

Wood sorrel is a plant principally of ancient deciduous woods, but it can tolerate the shade and acid soils of evergreen plantations better than many species, and often survives coniferisation. On the otherwise dark and barren floors the leaves of wood sorrel can appear an almost luminous viridian. They lie in scattered clusters amongst the needles like fretwork. Gerard Manley Hopkins described the new leaves as having the sharp appearance of green lettering. They are folded to begin with, in the shape of an Episcopal hat, then open flat, three hearts with their points joined at the stem.

The leaves of wood sorrel have an agreeably sharp, fruity taste, a little like the skins of young grapes, and were in use as a vegetable as early as the 14th Century. By the 15th Century wood sorrel was under cultivation, and in the 17th Century John Evelyn was recommending it in a list of the plants most suitable for the kitchen garden.

Its leaves were used then as an ingredient for salads, or pulped with sugar as a sauce for meats and fish. They can be used in the same way today, and their lemony tang gives them a special affinity with tomatoes. Hugh Fearnley-Whittingstall finds they also go well sprinkled on most cooked fungi dishes. But use them sparingly, as they contain oxalic acid, which is not good for the body in large quantities.

In the United States, other members of the *Oxalis* family (such as the yellow-flowered *Oxalis stricta*, also naturalised in Britain) are widely used, especially as flavourings for cakes.

DESCRIPTION
Low, creeping and
downy.

LEAVES
rounded.

FLOWERS
blue-violet or white,
March–May.

HABITAT
woods, hedgebanks,
cultivated in gardens
throughout Europe.

Sweet Violet
Viola odorata

A native of woods and hedgebanks, much cultivated in gardens, and escaped and naturalised far beyond its native range. Its flowers, deep mauve or white, are bigger and squarer than those of other common violet species and are pleasantly fragrant (though the scent appears to be ephemeral because of its slight anaesthetising effect on smell receptors in the nose).

Sweet violet flowers (and their quite large, heart-shaped leaves) were an ingredient of the elaborate Elizabethan salads known as Grand Salletts, or Salmagundies. In the 14th Century they were beaten up with a ground rice pudding flavoured with ground almonds and cream (they still make a fine flavouring for rice puddings).

They are best known, though, as crystallised or candied sweets. The latter are easy to make by picking the flowers with the stem attached, dipping them first in beaten egg white and then into a bowl of fine granulated sugar. Use a small paintbrush to coat difficult cavities, as it is important to cover every part with sugar to preserve the flower properly. Then let the flowers dry for a few days on greaseproof paper before storing in a tight container in the refrigerator.

Cow Parsley
Anthriscus sylvestris

DESCRIPTION
Erect, leafy, branched
perennial is usually about
1m (3ft) high, with
hollow, green, furrowed
stems, hairy near the
bottom of the plant, but
smooth above.

LEAVES
grass-green, slight downy,
and much divided,
resembling wedge-shaped
ferns.

FLOWERS
umbels of tiny white
flowers, April–June.

HABITAT
waysides, in pastures and
woods. Widespread and
abundant across most of
Europe.

No plant shapes our roadside landscape more than cow parsley. In May its lacy white flowers teem along every path and hedgebank. It grows prolifically; road verges can be blanketed with it for miles on end, and be broadened several feet by its overhanging foliage.

This provident plant has been almost totally overlooked as a herb, even though one of its less common botanical names is wild chervil. It is in fact the closest wild relative of cultivated chervil, *Anthriscus cerefolium*, a little coarser than that garden variety, maybe, but sharing the same fresh, spicy flavour.

Cow parsley is the first common umbelliferate to come into flower in the spring, and this is often enough to identify it positively. But since there are a number of related species which resemble it, and which can cause serious poisoning, I have included below some notes on the characteristics

which unequivocally identify cow parsley. The most dangerous sources of confusion are fool's parsley and hemlock, and it is with these plants in mind that I have selected the criteria. I must stress, however, that these few pointers are in no way a substitute for a well-illustrated field guide, they are merely intended to bring out the most prominent and useful differentiating characteristics.

In addition hemlock has an offensive, mousey smell when any part of it is bruised, and fool's parsley has unmistakable drooping green bracts growing beneath the flowers, giving them a rather bearded appearance.

You should pick wild chervil as soon as the stems are sufficiently

ABOVE
Hemlock, *Conium
maculatum*.

Species	Size	Stem
Cow Parsley	Up to 1.2m (4ft)	Stout, pale-green, furrowed, slightly hairy
Fool's Parsley	Up to 0.5m (12in)	Thin, hairless, ribbed, hollow
Hemlock	Up to 2.1m (7ft)	Stout, smooth, purple-spotted

developed for you to identify it. Later in the year it becomes rather bitter. It dries well, so pick enough to last you through the off-season as well as for your immediate needs. But do not gather the plant from the sides of major roads where it will certainly have been contaminated by car exhausts.

Chervil is a very versatile herb and small quantities make a lively addition to most sorts of salads, particularly cold potato, tomato, and cucumber. It also makes a good flavouring for hot haricot beans, and with chopped chives, tarragon and parsley, the famous 'omelettes fines herbes'.

A second crop of non-flowering leaves often appears in the autumn and remains green throughout the winter, and those experienced enough to tell the plant from its leaves alone could do worse than pick some fresh for winter soups and casseroles. It goes well with hot baked potatoes, and as an addition to the French country dish, cassoulet.

DESCRIPTION
hairless perennial
forming large patches
30–100cm (12–40in)
high.

FLOWERS
white umbels on a
creeping, hairless stem,
June–August.

LEAVES
finely toothed, in groups
of three at the end of the
leaf stems.

HABITAT
shady waste places, on
roadsides and under
hedges. Widespread
throughout Europe.

Ground Elder, Goutweed

Aegopodium podagraria

Though no relation of the elder, goutweed's leaves do bear a superficial resemblance to those of the common and similarly prolific shrub. It can often be found in quite large patches by roadsides and under garden hedges, its slightly crinkly pale green leaves making a bright carpet in shady places. Its continued presence in both habitats is a telling example of the persistence of some plants in places where they were once cultivated – or discarded.

Ground elder was probably introduced to Britain by the Romans. In the Middle Ages it was grown in gardens as a vegetable, and at roadside inns and monasteries as a supposed quick palliative for travellers' gout. Advances in medical understanding put paid to the second of these functions, and the growing preference for milder tasting, fuller-leaved vegetables to the first. Any popularity ground elder might have retained was finally undermined by the colonial tendencies of its rootstock, which could rapidly take over its host's garden. Even in the 16th Century, when the plant was still being used as a pot-herb, John Gerard wrote complainingly of it that:

> 'once taken roote, it will hardly be gotten out again, spoiling
> and getting every yeere more ground, to the annoying of better
> herbes',

– a sentiment which many modern gardeners will echo. In fact one way of getting back at the invader is to eat it. Cooked like a spinach, for about five minutes, it makes an unusual vegetable. Its tangy, aromatic flavour, though, is not to everyone's taste, so it is as well to try it in small quantities first.

DESCRIPTION
Low, hairy perennial
10–35cm (4–14in).

LEAVES
narrow at the base.

FLOWERS
yellow with orange spots
in the centre, 10–15mm,
between 1 and 30 flowers
in a cluster, April–May.

HABITAT
road verges, chalk downs
and meadowland.
Widespread, local in
Scotland.

Cowslip
Primula veris

The cheerful wobbly, blossoms of the cowslip have made it one of our favourite flowers, for ornament and cooking, and in recent years it has suffered from over-picking as well as from the spraying and ploughing of its favourite habitats on chalk downs and meadowland. Yet its name hardly suggests such popularity. It is a euphemism for 'cowslop', no doubt an indication of the plant's liking for mucky meadows.

It was once widely used in kitchens, making one of the best country wines, and a curious 'vinegar' which was drunk with soda water rather than being used as a condiment. (It required two pints of blooms to make a pint and half of vinegar, which shows the strain some of these recipes must have put on wild populations.) Izaak Walton used cowslip flowers as a flavouring for minnows, as described in *The Compleat Angler*, (fifth edition, 1676):

'*He is a sharp biter at a small worm, and in hot weather makes excellent sport for young anglers, or boys, or women that love that recreation, and in the spring they make of them excellent minnow-tansies: for being washed well in salt, and their heads and tails cut off, and their guts taken out, and not washed after, they prove excellent for that use; that is, being fried with yolks of eggs, the flowers of cowslips, and of primroses, and a little tansy; thus used they make a dainty dish of meat.*'

Warning

The picking of wild spring flowers is strongly discouraged these days because of their declining populations, though they have been anciently popular ingredients of salads. If you like the sound of any of the recipes below, grow the plants in your garden, and pick the flowers there.

DESCRIPTION
A bushy, hairy perennial
50–120cm (20–47in).

LEAVES
dark green, hairy, spear-
shaped.

FLOWERS
white, cream, pink or
mauve bellflowers in
clusters, May–October.

HABITAT
waste ground, river
banks, waysides and
waste ground, sometimes
forming large colonies.
Widespread and common
throughout Europe.

Common Comfrey
Symphytum officinale

Comfrey is an increasingly common plant of damp places, especially by running water. In this sort of habitat its broad, spear-shaped leaves are unmistakable, even when the plant is not in bloom. They are dull and hairy underneath, a fine, dark, almost glossy green above, and with slightly indented reticulations, as if the leaves had been pressed against a mould.

It is the leaves which are now used in cookery. Don't worry about their

furry texture as this disappears completely during cooking. Nor is there much need to be particular about the age of the leaves you use, for in my experience the older ones (provided of course they have not started to wither) have more flavour than the younger. One way of using them is to boil them like spinach, with plenty of seasoning. There is no need to add butter, as the leaves themselves are fairly glutinous. The young leaf spears, picked in March when they are no more than a few centimetres tall, make excellent salads, not unlike sliced cucumber.

Comfrey (from the Latin *confervere*, to grow together) was the medieval herbalists' favourite bone-setter. The root was lifted in the spring, grated up and used as plaster is today. In a short while the mash would set as solid as a hardwood. In fact the whole plant was one of those 'wonder herbs' that was used for every sort of knitting operation from drawing splinters to healing ruptures.

Gerard's recommendation was even more eclectic:

> *'The slimie substance of the roote made in a posset of ale, and given to drinke against the paine in the backe, gotten by any violent motion, as wrestling, or over much use of women, doth in fower or five daies perfectly cure the same ...'*

Schwarzwurz

The best recipe for comfrey leaves is a Teutonic fritter called Schwarzwurz.

Comfrey leaves, as many as required
1 egg
50g (2oz) plain flour
250ml (½ pint) milk or water
¼ teaspoon sea salt
Butter or oil for frying

1 Leave the stalks on the comfrey leaves, wash well, and dip into a thin batter made from the egg, flour and milk or water.

2 Fry the battered leaf in oil for not more than two minutes. For a more succulent result stick two or three similarly-sized leaves together before battering. The crisp golden batter contrasts delightfully with the mild, glutinous leaves.

3 They make an excellent, succulent companion to fried fish, which echo the shape of the leaves.

DESCRIPTION
Low, hairy perennial
10–25cm (4–10in).

LEAVES
taper to stalk.

FLOWERS
pale yellow 2–4cm
(1–2in), March–May.

HABITAT
woods, hedgebanks,
railway embankments,
meadows and cliffs.
Widespread throughout
Europe.

Primrose
Primula vulgaris

The *prima rosa*, first flower and symbol of spring, is widespread in woods, hedgebanks, railway embankments, meadows and on cliffs, especially on richer soils – though it is often scarce close to towns and other built-up areas because of uprooting.

Primroses have been used in similar ways to violets and cowslips – strewn on salads and on roast meats, candied and made into wine, but they are not common enough in most places today to justify picking from the wild.

Ground Ivy

Glechoma hederacea

DESCRIPTION
A low, creeping perennial, often carpeting the ground 10–50cm (4–20in).

LEAVES
kidney-shaped, long-stalked, softly hairy.

FLOWERS
blue, in whorls at the base of the leaves, March–June.

HABITAT
woods, hedges, cultivated ground. Common throughout Europe.

The dried leaves of ground ivy make one of the more agreeable herbal teas, cooling and with a sharp, slight fragrance. Before hops became widely accepted in the 17th Century, ground ivy-known – then as alehoof – was one of the chief agents for flavouring and clarifying ale. Culpeper wrote of it:

'It is good to tun up with new drink, for it will clarify it in a night, that it will be fitter to be dranke the next morning; or if any drinke be thick with removing or any other accident, it will do the like in a few hours.'

DESCRIPTION
Medium hairy perennial.

LEAVES
yellow-green, pointed, oval; lowest are heart-shaped.

FLOWERS
white or pale yellow in leafy whorls, 1–1.5cm (½–1in), July–September.

HABITAT
hedgebanks and shady places. Naturalised in southern England.

Balm
Melissa officinalis

A Mediterranean herb, with strongly lemon-scented leaves, introduced and widely naturalised in waste places and near gardens in southern Britain. Balm is an undistinguished-looking plant like a bushy mint, yet it has always been popular in herb gardens. Bees adore the flowers and it was reputed that they would never leave a garden that included them. While a bee-hive was still a standard fixture in cottage gardens, so was 'bee-balm' one of its commoner vernacular names.

Balm is still grown for its lemon-scented leaves, which make a refreshing tea; make an infusion of fresh leaves and stalks, strain and drink as it is, or add ice to make a cooler for hot days. Frah or dried leaves can also be added to light Indian or China teas for extra flavour and for their positive medicinal effects. It has a gentle calming action that can relieve tension; extracts and essential oils also have healing properties.

Leaves can also be added to wine-cups, or they can form a substitute for lemons in stuffings and salads, and can be used to give a tang to apple jelly.

DESCRIPTION
Medium-sized perennial,
almost hairless.

LEAVES
toothed, pinnate.

FLOWERS
yellow, button-like in
large clusters,
July–October.

HABITAT
grassy and waste places
throughout Europe

Tansy

Chrysanthemum vulgare

There was a time when tansy was one of the most widely-grown garden herb of all. It was a key item in the housewife's armoury of medicines, and had an extraordinarily wide range of uses in the kitchen. All of which goes to show how much our tastes have changed over the last few centuries, for even by the fairly tolerant standards I have tried to apply in this book, tansy is an unusually off-putting plant. It smells like a strong chest-ointment and has a hot, bitter taste. Used in excess it is more than unpleasant, and can be a dangerous irritant to the stomach.

Nevertheless, at Easter the young leaves were traditionally served with fried eggs and used to flavour puddings made from milk, flour and eggs. This may have been to symbolise the bitter herbs eaten by the Jews at Passover, though one 16th-Century writer explained that it was to counteract the effects 'engendered of Fish in the Lent season'. He may have been on to

something, as the quality of fish at that time no doubt gave much room for the development of worms, and Oil of Tansy is quite effective as a vermifuge.

Earlier still, the juice was extracted from the chopped leaves and used to flavour omelettes. This gave the name 'Tansye' in the 15th Century as a generic term for any herb-flavoured omelette. And there was a delightful medieval bubble-and-squeak, made from a fry-up of tansy leaves, green corn, and violets, and served with orange and sugar. Try the taste of tansy for yourself. Whatever you think of its flavour it is an attractive little plant with its golden, button-shaped flowers and ferny leaves.

DESCRIPTION
A bulbous perennial, growing up to 50cm (20in).

LEAVES
broad and spear-like, often carpeting large areas from early March.

FLOWERS
white and star-like in a rounded umbel, April–June.

HABITAT
damp woods and hedgebanks. Widespread and locally abundant throughout most of Europe.

Ramsons, Wild Garlic

Allium ursinum

Large colonies of ramsons can often be smelt from some distance away, and garlic woods sometimes figured as landmarks in old land charters. But the taste of the leaf is milder than you might expect, and it makes an excellent substitute for garlic or spring onion in salads. The woodland ecologist Oliver Rackham enjoys them added to peanut butter sandwiches during fieldwork.

For use in salads or sauces simply cut the leaves crosswise. Also try the leaves chopped in sour cream or mayonnaise. Or take advantage of their size, cut them into long strips to lay criss-cross over sliced beef tomatoes. They have an affinity with tomatoes and one Italian chef in the Chilterns (who also makes flavoured olive oil by soaking ramsons leaves in it) sometimes adds them to tomato sauces instead of basil.

Several other species of the garlic and onion family occur wild or naturalised in Britain, and the young leaves can be chopped and used as chives. Three-cornered leek, *Allium triquetrum*, with white bell-flowers and triangular stems is quite commonly naturalised in the South-west. Crow garlic, *A. vineale*, is frequent in arable fields and on waysides. Small, pearly bulbils form at the top of the stems which can also be gathered and added to dishes, or kept for a fortnight in water or damp paper, and used in 'sprouting salads'. Chives itself, *A. schoenoprasum*, also crops up here and there as a naturalised escape, as do cultivated onions and leeks.

ABOVE RIGHT
Allium ursinum

ABOVE LEFT
Allium shoenoprasum

DESCRIPTION
Medium-tall hairless
perennial.

LEAVES
greyish, basal, linear.

FLOWERS
greenish-white or
yellowish, 6-petalled in
tall spikes, May–July.

DISTRIBUTION
local and restricted.

HABITAT
bare and grassy places.

Bath Asparagus, Spiked Star-of-Bethlehem

Ornithogalum pyrenaicum

A member of the lily family whose tall spikes of greenish-yellow flowers area are distinctive feature of the limestone country around Bath and in the Avon Valley in May and June. The young unopened flower spikes were

gathered from woods and hedgebanks and sold in the local markets for cooking as asparagus (a near relative). The species is too scarce and local to justify this kind of harvest today, though a few people keep up the custom on private land and it remains one of the more historically interesting wild foods.

Ornithogalum pyrenaicum is strictly a Mediterranean native; its distribution in Britain is concentrated in the counties of Avon and Wiltshire (although small colonies do occur elsewhere). It is a very common sight in this area, particularly near Bradford-on Avon, and in spring can be almost as numerous as the bluebell. Indeed, there has been some speculation that it abundance round Bath may be a legacy of the Roman occupation of the area, either accidentally, or as a deliberate introduction.

DESCRIPTION
Very tall perennial, forms
dense beds.

LEAVES
broad, 1–2cm (½–1in).

HABITAT
still, shallow water in
marshes, woods, fens and
water edges.

Reed
Phragmites australis

When the stems of this familiar waterside plant are still green and are broken in some way they slowly exude a sugary substance which eventually hardens into a gum. Native North Americans used to collect this and break it into balls, which they chewed as sweets. Another Amerindian way with the plant was to cut the reeds whilst green, dry them, grind them and sift out the flour. This contains so much sugar that when it was placed near a fire it melted, swelled and was eaten like toasted marshmallow.

Early Purple Orchid

Orchis mascula

It would be irresponsible (and illegal in most cases) to dig up any of the dwindling colonies of early purple orchid. Yet when it was much more common it provided one of the most fascinating of wild foods.

The tubers contain a highly nutritious starch-like substance called bassorine, and it is these that have been used domestically, especially in the Middle East. In Turkey they are dug up after the plant has flowered, and made into a drink called *Sahlep*. For this the tubers are dried in the sun and ground into a rough flour. This is mixed with cinnamon and honey, and stirred into hot milk until it thickens.

In Britain, an almost identical drink called Saloop was popular before the spread of coffee. In Victorian books it is mentioned as a tea-break beverage of manual workers. Charles Lamb refers to a 'Salopian shop' in Fleet Street, and suggested that, at a cost of just three half-pence, a basin of Saloop, accompanied by a slice of bread and butter (costing a halfpenny), made a good breakfast for a chimney-sweep. They made it with water more often than milk, sometimes lacing it with spirits, sometimes brewing it so thick it had to be eaten with a spoon.

Most of it was made with tubers imported from Turkey, but Charles Bryant suggested in *Flora Diaetetica* (1783) how native stock might be used instead, underlining how well-known and widespread the plant was in the 18th Century:

'As most country people are acquainted with these plants, by the name of Cuckoo-flowers, it certainly would be worth their while to employ their children to collect the roots for sale; and though they may not be quite so large as those that come from abroad, yet they may be equally as good, and as they are exceedingly plentiful, enough might annually be gathered for our consumption, and thus a new article of employment would be added to the poorer sort of people … all the trouble of preparing them is, to put them fresh taken up into scalding hot water for about half a minute; and on taking them out rub off the outer skin; which done, they must be laid on tin plates, and set in a pretty fierce oven for eight or ten minutes, according to

the size of the roots; after this, they should be removed to the top of the oven, and let there till they are dry enough to pound.'

Bryant mentions Saloop's reputation as a 'restorative' but it was also regarded as an aphrodisiac (a sympathetic magic belief based on the twin tubers' resemblance to testicles). In the more fruitful days of the 17th Century, Robert Turner was moved to remark that enough orchids grew in Cobham Park in Kent to pleasure all the seamen's wives in Rochester. And the august College of Physicians published an extraordinary recipe in their *Pharmacopoeia* as 'a Provocative to Venery'. A rather long list of ingredients included orchid tubers, dates, bitter almonds, Indian nuts, pine nuts, pistachio nuts, candied ginger, candied Eryngo root, clover, galingale, peppers, ambergris, musk, penid (barley sugar), cinnamon, saffron, Malaga wine, nutmeg, grains of Paradise, ashkeys, the 'belly and loins of scinks', borax, benzoin, wood of aloes, cardamons, nettle seed and avens root.

Seaweeds

Although they reproduce by spores, not flowers, seaweeds have seasons of growth like other plants. They produce shoots in the spring, grow quickly and luxuriantly during the summer, and wither in the winter. The best months to gather most seaweeds are May and June.

Seaweeds obtain their food entirely from the surrounding sea water and do not have roots in the conventional sense. However they do have hold-fasts, by which they attach themselves to rocks and stones, and from which the stem-like part, or stipe, grows. The weed itself can regenerate from a cut stipe, provided the cut is not too near the hold-fast. So if you

are cutting seaweed rather than gathering leaves which have been washed free of their moorings, leave plenty of stipe so that the weed can grow again.

Before cooking any seaweed always wash thoroughly in fresh water to remove sand, shells and other shoreline debris which may have stuck to it.

Seaweeds are rich in minerals, particularly iodides, and you may take a little while to get used to their flavours. But do give them a fair chance; they are intriguing foods, and quite undeserving of their joke-book reputation.

DESCRIPTION
Inflated tube, irregularly constricted, to 75cm (30in) long. Pale to dark green.

HABITAT
abundant on salt marshes and in dikes and rocky pools.

Gutweed
Enteromorpha intestinalis

(See photograph above.) A member of the class Chorophycaea, or green seaweeds, which really are green as their cholorophyll is not disguised by other pigments. Pick in the early spring, and stir-fry until crisp.

DESCRIPTION
Broad, tough, crumpled
frond 10–30cm (4–12in)
across; attached to stones
and rocks.

**DISTRIBUTION AND
HABITAT**
quite common at all tidal
levels, especially in
places where water runs
into the sea.

Sea Lettuce
Ulva lactuca

One of the more pleasant seaweeds served raw, especially chopped, and served Japanese style, with soy sauce and rice vinegar.

DESCRIPTION
Frond is characterised by
prominent midrib and
pairs of gas bladders up to
1m (3ft) long. Dark olive
brown.

HABITAT
Abundant on the middle
shore, into estuaries.

Bladder Wrack, Popweed
Fucus vesiculosus

This species can be washed, simmered in a little water and served as a green vegetable.

DESCRIPTION
Up to 2m(6ft); long
stem, broad blade splits
into fingers as it matures
(can be up to 10).

HABITAT
often found attached to
small stones on muddy
and sandy flats.

Oarweed, Tangle
Laminaria digitata

The young stipes of this weed (see photograph below left) used to be sold
in Scotland under the name of 'tangle'. One writer describes their taste as
resembling that of peanuts. A jelly, made from this weed and dulse and
called *Pain des Algues*, used to be prepared on the coast of Armorica.

DESCRIPTION
Short, slender stem,
ribbon-like blade with
crinkled edges, up to 4m
(13ft) long.

HABITAT
low-water mark on rocky
shores all round the
coast.

Sea Belt, Poor Man's Weather Glass
Laminaria saccarina

(See photograph above right.) As well as a salad vegetable, this weed is
used as a source of alginates.

DESCRIPTION
Short stem, narrow,
slightly wavy blade
0.5–3m (1½–10ft) long.
Fronds may appear
feathery. Yellowish-olive
to reddish-brown.

HABITAT
North Sea, northern
Atlantic coasts.

Dabberlocks
Alaria esculenta

This species occurs on exposed shores where it takes the place of *Laminaria
digitata* (see above).

Dulse
Palmaria palmata

DESCRIPTION
A tough, flat frond
10–30cm (4–12in) long.
Dark red, but can look
purple underwater.

HABITAT
abundant on stones on
the middle and lower
shores. North Sea,
northern Atlantic coasts.

Also known as *Rhodymenia palmata*, dulse (see photograph below) has been eaten raw as a salad, and in New England the dried fronds are used as a relish. It is also accasionally grazed by sheep and cattle. It is a very tough weed, and as a cooked vegetable needs up to five hours simmering.

Pepper Dulse
Laurencia pinnatifida

DESCRIPTION
An infrequent weed
which forms dense tufts.
Flattened fronds;
alternate branches divide
into smaller branchlets.
Size variable 7–20cm
(3–8in) depending on
habitat. Brownish-
purple; lighter in bright
areas.

HABITAT
rock crevices on the
middle shore.

Pepper dulse is very pungent and is usually used as a condiment. In Iceland it has been employed as a substitute for chewing tobacco.

DESCRIPTION
Grows in clusters of purple-brown fronds. These have a distinctly flat stalk, and branch repeatedly into a rough fan shape.

HABITAT
widespread on stones and rocks on temperate Atlantic shores.

Carragheen, Irish Moss

Chondrus crispus

In the class Rhodophyceae, or red seaweeds, the green of chloropyll is maked by a red pigment. They appear in a variety of colours ranging from brown to bright pink. These weeds are multi-cellular and often small in size; the fronds of Carragheen are usually 5–15cm (3–6in) in length.

Carragheen is an important source of alginates – vegetable gelatines – which are used for thickening soups, emulsifying ice-creams and setting jellies. They can also be made into thin, durable films for use as edible sausage skins.

You can find carragheen on almost any western or southern shore, although like other red seaweeds, it does not tolerate brackish conditions. It is best gathered young, in April or May, and either used immediately or carefully dried. To use the weed fresh, wash it well, add one cup of weed to three cups of milk or water, and add sugar and flavouring to taste. Then simmer slowly until most of the weed has dissolved. Remove any undissolved fragments and pour into a mould to set. This produces a basic carragheen blancmange or jelly, depending on whether you use milk or water. Ginger makes a good flavouring, and can be added in the form of the chopped root, or as ground powder, during the simmering of the weed.

To dry the weed, wash it well, and then lay out to dry on a wind-free surface out-of-doors. Wash it from time to time with fresh water, or simply leave it in the rain. After a while it will become bleached to a creamy-white colour. Trim off any tough stalks, dry thoroughly indoors, and then store in bags. The dried weed can be used exactly as if it were fresh.

Carragheen grows abundantly in the Channel Islands and during the war it was gathered and sold in shops. The demand was so great that boats had to be used in spite of the large number of mines in the area. The weed was used to thicken soups and stews.

Gigartina stellata, common and often abundant on the middle and lower shore, especially on the West coast, can be used to provide jelly bases for a number of dishes, like carragheen.

ABOVE
Although usually red, carragheen looks green in bright light

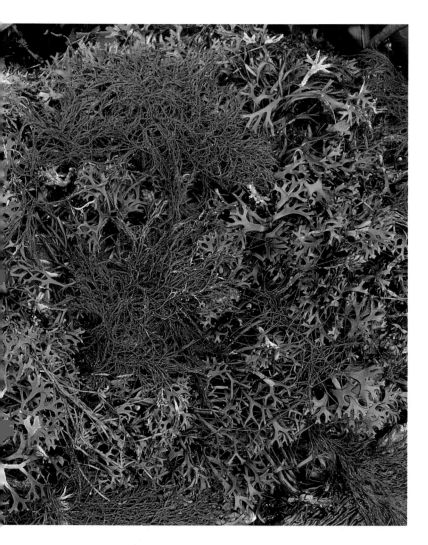

DESCRIPTION
Broad, tough, thin, irregular purple frond, 20cm (8in) across. Greenish when young, becoming purplish-red.

HABITAT
grows on rock and stones at most levels of the beach, especially where the stones are likely to be covered with sand. Common all round Britain, especially on exposed shores on the west coast.

Purple Laver
Porphyra umbilicalis

In the south-west of Wales, laver is considered a great delicacy, and it sells briskly in many food shops to those who don't want the bother of gathering it for themselves. Yet it is one of the easier seaweeds to find and recognise, its translucent purple fronds liable to crop up on almost all levels of the shore. In Japan it is cultivated. Bundles of bamboo are placed on the sea bottom, just offshore, and transferred to fresh river water once the weed has established itself. In these conditions the laver apparently grows softer and more extensive fronds. The Chinese and Japanese make very varied use of their laver, in soups and stews, as a covering for round rice balls, and in pickles and preserves.

In Britain there have been two classic, traditional uses: laver sauce for mutton, and laverbread. The first stage in any laver recipe is to reduce the weed to a sort of rough purée. First wash it well and then simmer in a little water until it is like well-cooked spinach. This is best done in a double saucepan as the laver sticks easily. This mush, if transferred to a jar, will keep well for several days.

It is this purée which is sold in Wales under the name of laverbread. It ends up in the place you would least expect it – on the breakfast table, rolled in oatmeal and fried in bacon fat. To make laver sauce, beat up two cupfuls of the purée with 25g (1oz) of butter and the juice of one Seville orange.

A number of seaweeds can be cooked like laver and used as a vegetable, including all those illustrated in this section, and also *Monostroma grevillei* and *Irideaea edulis*.

Morel

Morchella esculenta

DESCRIPTION
Cap covered in deep, honeycomb-like pits; cap and stem form one continuous chamber.

CAP
variable, but usually globular in shape, 3–6cm (1–2in), deeply pitted. Colour ranges from light to dark brown. Brittle in texture.

GILLS
cap is fused to the stem

RING
none

HABITAT
woodland clearings, old orchards and pastures (especially sandy soils); under broad-leaved trees, especially ash and elm. March–May.

A fungus of great reputation and long standing, though now sadly rare. Its grows from March to May in woodland clearings, old orchards and on pastures, especially on sandy soils, overlying chalk. It also has a liking for burnt places, and there are records of colonies springing up on bomb sites in the war. In Germany, in the 18th Century, peasant women reputedly went to the lengths of starting forest fires to encourage the growth of morels.

The morel is distinctive, having a cap which resembles a cross-section of a honeycomb. The deep pitting of the club-shaped heads is the feature which differentiates true morel species from the false morels. One speciesd to avoid is *Gyromitra esculenta* or false morel which is poisonous; remember that the stem of the true morel is single-chambered, while the false morel is multi-chambered like the cap.

The pitted cap also means that morels have a habit of accumulating insects and detritus in their cavities, and need a good washing (or dusting with a paint brush) before use. They are sometimes blanched in boiling water before cooking. Morels make good additions to soups and stews, and being hollow they can also be stuffed and baked. Sliced horizontally they produce crinkle-edged golden rings that can ornament omelettes or mushroom soups.

Morels only appear for a few days each spring, often after warm rains, and if you are lucky enough to find a hoard it is worth preserving them. They freeze well, in airtight plastic bags, or can be dried. Cut them in half vertically and hang up in a warm room until they are crisp.

DESCRIPTION
A creamy-white fungus, with a fleshy cap with wavy edges.

CAP
fleshy and dense, 5–12cm (2–5in) when young, later flatter with wavy edges. Cap, gill and stem all creamy-white.

GILLS
creamy-white, crowded.

RING
none

HABITAT
among grass on open pasture, roadside verges, lawns and woodland margins. April–June.

St George's Mushroom

Tricholoma gambosum

This is the French 'mousseron', unmistakable as the only large white mushroom to appear in spring – traditionally around St George's Day, 23 April. It likes old grassland – chalk downland, grassy woodland edges and even churchyards. It is creamy white in all parts, which is usually enough to identify it early in the year, and has a strong, mealy, almost yeasty smell that some may find too rich (though this is less pronounced in younger specimens).

St George's mushrooms are firm, not often attacked by insects and can generally be treated like field mushrooms. But, because of their strong flavour they are probably best used in dishes where there is another strongly flavoured ingredient – for instance in quiches with cheese and spinach or spring greens.

Fairy-ring Champignon
Marasmius oreades

DESCRIPTION
Smells pleasantly aromatic, a little like new-mown hay scented with bitter almonds.

CAP
2–5cm (1–2in) slight bump in the centre. When moist, the top is smooth and buffish in colour, and when dry, the skin wrinkles, becomes hard and leathery and changes to pale tan in colour.

GILLS
wide and usually free of the stipe (3–8cm, 2–3in), which is tough and fibrous.

HABITAT
very common on lawns and short grassland, often growing in 'fairy rings'. April–December.

This is one of the best and most versatile toadstools – though care must be taken to distinguish it from somewhat similar small, white and poisonous *Clitocybe* species that can grow on lawns.

The fairy-ring champignon's natural tendency to dry out is one of its great virtues, and means that the caps can be easily preserved by threading them on to strings and hanging for a week or two in a dry, well-ventilated room. Discard the tough stems before threading. They can be reconstituted by soaking in water overnight.

The other virtues of the fairy-ring champignon are their almond fragrance and nutty texture; they are prized for their flavour rather than their bulk. Add them to stews and casseroles – or fry them with chopped almonds or hazelnuts.

SUMMER

The cresses on the water and the sorrels are at hand,

And the cuckoo's calling daily his note of music bland,

And the bold thrush sings so bravely his song i' the forests grand,

On the fair hills of holy Ireland.

THE FAIR HILLS OF IRELAND, Donnchad Ruadh MacNamara (translated by Samuel Ferguson), written c.1730

DESCRIPTION
A tall, deciduous tree, up
to 46m (150ft), when it
allowed to grow
naturally, with a dark
brown trunk interrupted
by bosses and side shoots.

LEAVES
large and heart-shaped,
smooth above, paler
below with a few tufts of
fine white hairs.

FLOWERS
drooping clusters of
heavily scented yellow
blossom, July.

HABITAT
frequent in parks, by
roadsides and in
ornamental woods.

RIGHT
Common lime, *Tilia
europaea*

Common Lime
Tilia europaea

The common lime is a cultivated hybrid between the two species of native
wild lime, small-leaved, *Tilia cordata*, and large-leaved, *T. platyphyllos*, and
is now much commoner than both. It is one of the most beneficent of trees.
Its branches are a favourite site for mistletoe. Its inner bark, bast, was used
for making twine. Its pale, close-grained timber is ideal for carving, and its
fragrant flowers make one of the best honeys. Limes are remarkable for the
fact that they can, in flower, be tracked down by sound. In high summer
their flowers are often so laden with bees that they be heard 50m (160ft)
away.

The leaves make a useful salad vegetable. When young they are thick,
cooling and very glutinous. Before they begin to roughen they can be used
as a sandwich filling, between slices of crisp new bread, with unsalted butter
and just a sprinkling of lemon juice. Some aficionados enjoy them when
they are sticky with the honeydew produced by aphid invasions in the
summer.

But lime's most important use in the kitchen is as the source of lime blossom tea, one of the most sumptuous and beautifully coloured of all tisanes. It is popular in France where it is sold under the name of tilleul. (Once, at a restaurant in the Herault district renowned for its extravagant courtesies to guests, I was served tilleul made from the blossoms of the particular lime tree which sheltered the farmhouse where I was staying.)

The flowers should be gathered whilst they are in full bloom in June or early July, and laid out on trays or sheet of paper in a warm well-ventilated room. After two weeks they should have turned brittle and will be ready to use. Make tea in the usual way (without milk), experimenting with strengths. The tisane can have a sedative effect when strong, and was used by doctors during the Second World War as a mild tranquilliser.

One final oddity. During the 19th Century the French chemist Missa made what he regarded as a chocolate substitute by grinding up a mixture of lime flowers with lime fruits, the spherical capsules that follow in July and August. In fact the paste tastes nothing like chocolate but is an intriguing confection for all that.

LEFT
Large-leaved lime, *Tilia platyphyllos*

Juneberry
Amelanchier lamarckii

DESCRIPTION
Introduced, deciduous tree, up to 10m (33ft).

LEAVES
alternate, oblong, up to 8cm (3in).

FLOWERS
drifts of white blossom, April–May.

FRUIT
purplish-black/red, 1cm (½in), with withered sepals.

HABITAT
woodland.

An American shrub naturalised in woods in the south of England, notably on sandy soils in Sussex. The purplish-red berries rarely form in this country (in June when they do), but are sweet enough to be eaten raw in their native United States. They are also made into pies and canned for winter use.

A related species, the snowy mespilus, A. *ovalis*, is native in scrub and hill thickets in southern Europe, and has sweet, bluish-black berries.

Hottentot Fig
Cartobrotus edulis

DESCRIPTION
Trailing branched perennial.

LEAVES
fleshy.

FLOWERS
yellow, pint or magenta with yellow stamens.

FRUIT
fleshy, May–July.

HABITAT
clifftops

This garden plant from South Africa, better known by its old name of *Mesembyanthemum*, is now naturalised in the warm climate of Devon and Cornwall. There, near the sea, its matted, succulent foliage and silky pink flowers can breathe a hint of the tropics into the most stolid British cliff. Its fruits, the figs, are edible and pleasantly tangy.

DESCRIPTION
Succulent annuals,
varying from single
unbranched stems to
thick, stubby bushes up
to 30cm (12in) tall.
Stems are shiny and
jointed.

FLOWERS
minute, and only really
visible as one or two
white to red stamens
growing out of the
junctions in the stems.

HABITAT
common and often
abundant on saltmarshes
throughout Europe.

ABOVE
Marsh samphire on
mudflats with Snowdonia
beyond, Anglesea

Marsh Samphire, Glasswort

Salicornia spp

I have always had a particular affection for marsh samphire, since it was the plant which first made me aware that there was more to edible wild plants than picking blackberries and roasting chestnuts. But even in its won right it is something of a character. It is, for instance, one of the few wild vegetables to be sold commercially – but in fishmongers' shops, not greengrocers, laid out amongst the dabs and cockles like a dish of green eels. It is not hard to understand this, because samphire is a thoroughly maritime species, and has little in common with 'land' vegetables. It is one of the first colonisers of intertidal mudflats, and its bright green, jointed stalks can often cloak acres of glistening saltings and creeks.

Tradition has it that the stems can be picked from midsummer day, and that they are at their best and freshest when they are 'washed by every tide'. Picking in such circumstances brings out the absurd in all but the most reserved of souls. Samphire has a liking for such execrably muddy situations, and grows in such natural abundance on many saltmarshes that communal picking seems the most obvious and natural way to cope with it. You go out at low tide, with buckets and wellingtons, through the sea-aster and wormwood in the rough ground at the edge of the saltings, on to the tidal reaches where the crop grows. This is a world criss-crossed by deep and hidden creeks, by which you will be tripped, cut off and plastered up to the thigh with black wet mud. In these creeks samphire can grow tall and branched, like an amiable maritime cactus. After the 1953 floods in East Anglia, when all types of unconventional nutrients were washed into the marshes, a bush of samphire 2m (6ft) tall and as thick as a leek at the base was discovered in a creek near Blakeney. It was carried away on the crossbar of a bicycle and later hung up over the bar of a local pub.

On the sandier flats, the plants tend to grow as single shoots not much more than 20cm (8in) high. Yet they make up for this in sheer numbers. Often a bed can completely carpet several acres of marsh, and look as if it could be cut with shears – or a lawnmower. But there are no short cuts. Traditionally samphire was gathered by pulling up by the roots. This is illegal now, so there is no escaping half an hour in a stooping position,

Several other mashland plants can be gathered in the same season as samphire, and used either as a salad or cooked as spinach:

Sea purslane, *Halimione portulacoides* (see picture, right). The oval, fleshy, grey-green leaves make a succulent addition to salads.

Annual seablite, *Suaeda maritima*, blue-green annual, turning purplish in autumn. Can be eaten raw or cooked.

Several species of the orache and fat hen families, including common orache, *Atriplex patula*, and hastate orache, *A. hastata*, also favour the higher shoreline and can be treated like their relatives.

snipping the stems individually with a sharp knife or pair of scissors. But then hunched up and grubbing about in the mud is the true way to appreciate the delights of samphire gathering.

Collect the stems into a bucket, basket or best of all string bag, and rinse the bunch roughly in sea water to remove the worst of the mud before taking them home. Once you have the crop home, wash it well in fresh water, and remove the strands of seaweed and pieces of flotsam that will inevitably be stuck to some of the plants. But never leave samphire to stand in water for more than a few minutes. Its succulence is due to salt water stored by the plant, which will be sucked out by the fresh water and cause the plants to become limp and prone to decay. If you wish to keep the crop for a day or two, dry it well and store, unwrapped, in the fridge.

The succulence means that the young shoots picked in June or July make a crisp and tangy salad vegetable. Try chewing the sprigs straight from the marsh. They are very refreshing in spite of their salty taste. To cook, boil or steam in a little water for 8–10 minutes, drain and serve with melted butter. Eat by holding the stem at the base, dipping in the butter and sliding the stems between the teeth, to draw the flesh off the wiry central spine.

Samphire prepared like this can be served either as an asparagus-like starter, or as a vegetable with fish, poultry or lamb. Alternatively, for a culinary pun, cook together equal quantities of the tender tops of samphire and spaghetti, and serve as a kind of *paglia e fieno*, the Italian green and white noodle dish.

A traditional way with samphire is to pickle it. This was once done by filling jars with the chopped shoots, covering with spiced vinegar, and placing in a baker's oven as it cooled over the weekend. I would imagine that the result of 48 hours simmering would be on the sloppy side to say the least. To maintain the crisp texture and at least some of its brilliant green colour it is best to do no more than put it under cold pickling vinegar.

I have found pickled samphire being offered as a bar-top nibble in north Norfolk pubs in recent years, and there are signs that the plant is becoming more popular. It is appearing increasingly on the menus of metropolitan restaurants (though sometimes only as a garnish), and often imported from the continent, and the custom of selling it from a horse-drawn cart has been revived in Kings Lynn.

Carpaccio of salmon trout with samphire and seaweed puree

An adapted recipe for the original of which I am indebted to Dave Adlard of Adlard's Restaurant, Norwich.

900g (2lb) of smoked salmon trout, cut very thinly
1 lime
2 pieces of candied ginger, cut into fine strips
1 teaspoon of sugar
500g (1lb) of samphire (early crop to avoid the hard cores)
1 packet of Norri seaweed

1 Lay the fish in a circle on a large plate.

2 Boil the seaweed with water for five minutes

3 Blend in a food processor and pipe small dots around the salmon.

4 Sprinkle ginger, sugar, salt, pepper and the juice and zest of the lime over the fish.

5 In a frying pan quickly stir-fry the samphire. Arrange in the centre of the salmon trout.

Sea Kale
Crambe maritima

DESCRIPTION
A cabbage-like plant, growing in large clumps with huge grey-green leaves, very fleshy and glaucous.

FLOWERS
white and four-petalled, grow in a broad cluster, June–August.

HABITAT
Widespread but extremely local on sand and shingle by the sea. Throughout Europe, except the Mediterranean.

BELOW
Sea kale, Wylfa, Anglesea

I found my first sea kale through a pair of binoculars, on a barren stretch of North Norfolk shingle over 50 miles from the nearest record in the *Atlas of the British Flora*. It was the only plant in sight and was hunched over the sand like some heavy, stranded crustacean. Some of the leaves were nearly 0.6m (2ft) long, and had the texture of rubber sheet. They looked amazingly appetising, and I cut off a few for supper. They were so heavy and unwieldy that I had to improvise a driftwood and twine sling to get them home.

Now I must confess that all this was before I knew very much about the sea kale. I had read that it was prized as a delicacy and to me the fleshy green leaves seemed the most obvious part to use. That evening we boiled and boiled them, for nearly an hour and a half. They seemed quite immutable, changing colour a little, but holding that massive texture to the end. Eventually we ate them as they were. It was the most powerful and tangy taste I have ever experienced, like chewing the remains of a sunken battleship.

Later, of course, I learned that it was not the mature leaves that were normally eaten, but the young, white shoots. There is little doubt that in coastal areas the use of this part of the plant as a vegetable dates back centuries before it was taken into cultivation. In many areas on the south coast villagers would watch for the shoots to appear, pile sand and shingle round them to blanch out the bitterness and cut them in the summer to take to the markets in the nearest big town.

At this time sea kale was a relatively common plant around the coasts. But in 1799, the botanist William Curtis wrote a pamphlet called *Directions for the culture of the Crambe Maritima or Sea Kale, for the use of the Table*. As

a result the vegetable was taken up by Covent Garden, and demand for the naturally growing shoots increased greatly. This intensive collection was to have the effect of substantially reducing the population of wild sea kale.

Now the vegetable is out of fashion, but the wild plant shows no signs of regaining its former status. So be sparing if you do pick it, and do not take more than two or three stems from each plant. Use the lower parts of the leaf stalks, particularly any that you can find which have been growing under the ground. (They sometimes push their way through up to 1m (3ft) of shingle.) You could even adopt a local plant, and blanch the stems like coastal dwellers used to. If you object to heaps of shingle on the beach, cover the growing shoots with seaweed. However you grow them, when harvesting you will need a sharp knife to cut through the thick stems.

To cook sea kale, cut the stems and the young leaf shoots into manageable lengths, and steam or boil in water until tender (about 10–15 minutes). Then serve and eat with melted butter. The young flowers can also be cooked like broccoli.

Sea kale and pasta

Two handfuls of mixed stems, leaf shoots and small flower heads of sea kale.

500g (1lb) penne

Chopped anchovies

2 tablespoons olive oil

Butter

Lemon juice

1 Chop the sea kale into 5cm (2in) lengths and cook in boiling water for about ten minutes.

2 Add the penne to salted, boiling water and simmer until just cooked (8–10 minutes)

3 Drain the pasta, add the cooked sea kale, a few chopped anchovies, the olive oil, a knob of butter and a squeeze of lemon juice. Stir and heat for a further three minutes, and serve.

DESCRIPTION
Leafy, hairy perennial
50–120cm (20–47in).

LEAVES
pairs of large and smaller
leaflets, hairy undersides.

FLOWERS
creamy-white, frothy.

HABITAT
marshland, damp
grassland, woodland.

Meadowsweet

Filipendula ulmaria

One of the most summery of all our wild plants. In July the frothy flowerheads of meadowsweet can transform a heavy riverside meadow. As so often is the case, local names reveal a great deal about the flower's characteristics and uses. Courtship-and-Matrimony refers to the difference in scent before and after crushing the plant. So, the fresh flowers are warm and heady, the crushed leaves more clinically sharp. When dried, both parts of the plant smell of new-mown hay (hence the names Sweet Hay, Hayriff). It was these dried leaves that were used to give an especially aromatic bouquet to port, claret and mead, and it is to this function that the name Meadwort refers, not its preference for growing in meadows.

The leaves can be uses for flavouring many sorts of drink, and can double for woodruff if that plant is unobtainable.

DESCRIPTION
A nondescript little
plant, 10–50cm (4–20in)
high.

LEAVES
dark-green heart-shaped.

FLOWERS
small, white in loose,
domed clusters.

HABITAT
coastal cliffs, rocks and
salt-marshes, also walls
and banks.

Common Scurvy-grass
Cochlearia officinalis

Once famous as the major source of vitamin C on long sea voyages. It was taken on board in the form of dried bundles or distilled extracts. But it is an unpleasantly bitter plant, and the taste was often disguised with spices.

Sailors were not the only ones with reason to fear scurvy, and fads for early morning scurvy-grass drinks, and scurvy-grass sandwiches abounded right up till the middle of the 19th Century. It was only the ready availability of citrus fruits which finally made the plant obsolete.

Scurvy-grass still grows abundantly round cliffs and banks near the sea, and it was probably its convenient proximity that made it the favourite maritime anti-scorbutic.

DESCRIPTION
A native of western Asia,
now widely naturalised
on waste ground through
much of Europe.

LEAVES
large, slightly toothed,
crinkly and dock-like,
grow straight from the
ground to a height of
about 1m (3 ft).

FLOWERS
a shock of white
blossoms on a long spike,
May–September.

HABITAT
roadsides, railway
embankments, waste
ground.

Horseradish

Armoracia rusticana

Horseradish was brought to Britain from the near East in the 16th Century, specifically as a spice plant. Now it has spread across much of Britain, on roadsides, railway embankments, tips, even old brick piles, regenerating chiefly from pieces of broken root, and often quickly developing into large colonies.

There can be little mistaking its crinkly palm-like leaves, but if you are in any doubt, crush them between your fingers: they should have the characteristic horseradish smell. A spade (and the permission of the landowner) is imperative when gathering horseradish. The plant is a perennial, and carries an extensive an complex root system. You may need to dig quite deep and chop the woody structure to obtain a section for use. The exception is horseradish growing on light sandy soils, which grows very straight, and can usually be extracted by a simple straight pull.

The worst part of preparing horseradish is the peeling. Most sections are intractably knobbly, and will need considerable geometric skill before they can be reduced to a manageable state. Once they have been, the remains of the brown outer layer can be pared off with a sharp knife. This may be best done under water, as the sharp odour will have started to appear by now. (The prefix 'horse' means coarse, as in horse-mint.) You will be left with some pure white chunks of horseradish which need to be grated before they can be used. This is best done out of doors, as the fumes put the most blinding onions to shame.

The freshly grated root can be used as it stands, as a garnish for roast beef or smoked fish. But use it fairly soon after preparation, as it loses its potency in a couple of days. And under no circumstances compromise it by adding vinegar. If you do wish for a quickly-made sauce, whip the grated horseradish up with some plain yoghurt or creme fraiche, a little mustard, sugar and seasoning.

A more substantial and longer-lasting sauce is made this way: mix a teaspoon of dry mustard with a tablespoon of cold water, and blend until smooth. Combine with six heaped tablespoons of grated horseradish and salt and pepper. Allow to stand for a quarter of an hour. Then blend into a cupful of white sauce (or double cream if you do not want it to last especially long).

For a rampaging alternative, try the Universal Devil's Mixture:

> 'To devil the same, rub each piece over with the following mixture, having made a deep incision in any article of food that may be subjected to this Mephistophelian process. Put in a bowl a good tablespoonful of Durham mustard which mix with four tablespoonful of Chilli vinegar. Add to it a tablespoonful of grated horseradish, two bruised shallots, a teaspoonful of salt, half ditto of Cayenne, ditto of black pepper, and one of pounded sugar, two teaspoonsful of chopped chillies if handy. Add the yolks of two raw eggs. Take a paste brush, and after having slightly seasoned each piece with salt, rub over each piece with the same, probing some into the incisions. First broil slowly and then the last few minutes as near as possible to the Pandemonium fire.'

From *The Culinary Campaign*, Alexis Soyer, 1857

Salad Burnet
Sanguisorba minor

DESCRIPTION
Hairless perennial
20–90cm (8–35in).

LEAVES
4–12 pairs of oval,
toothed leaflets.

FLOWERS
green, reddish or purplish
May–August.

HABITAT
quite common in grassy
places on chalk.

When crushed the leaves of the salad burnet smell slightly of cucumber. They have long been used as an ingredient of salads, in spite of their diminutive size, and as a garnish for cooling summer drinks. In herb gardens of the past bacon recommended that salad burnet be planted with wild thyme and water mint 'to perfume the air most delightfully, being trodden on and crushed'.

Parsley Piert
Aphanes arvensis

DESCRIPTION
Very low, hairy, pale-
green annual.

LEAVES
lobed and toothed.

FLOWERS
tiny, green clusters,
April–October.

HABITAT
widespread and common
on arable and dry
ground.

The curious name of this plant probably derives from perce-pierre, a plant which breaks through stony ground. So, by sympathetic magic, it came to be used medicinally as a specific against kidney stones. Yet it was Culpeper of all people, herbal wizard extraordinary, who first recommended it as an honest domestic pickle.

Wild Rose, Dog Rose

Rosa canina

DESCRIPTION
A tall, sturdy shrub
1.2–3m (4–10ft) high,
with hooked prickles.

LEAVES
toothed.

FLOWERS
large, white to pink, five-
petalled, June–July.

HABITAT
widespread and common
in hedges, scrubland,
waste places, but less
frequent in Scotland.

The wild rose is England's national flower, and shows none of the protracted wilting often shown by garden roses, which can hang sodden and wrinkled on their branches for days. The wild rose has a simpler and less showy blossom which scarcely even droops before it sheds its petals. This is the stage when they should be gathered. Never pick or damage the young flowers. Towards the end of July, look for those that have already lost one or two petals, and then gently remove the others into your basket.

Wild roses have a more delicate scent than the garden varieties, but still some of that fleshy, perfumed texture. So if you have only a small quantity, use them neat in salads. Frances Perry once listed ten other uses for the petals: rose wine, rose in brandy, rose vinegar, rhubarb and rose-petal jam, rose honey, rose and coconut candies, Turkish delight, rose drops, crystallised rose petals, and rose-petal jelly. The use of rose petals, here as elsewhere, is simply as a fragrant improver of well-established dishes. Rose-petal jam is extensively eaten in the Middle East, especially with yoghurt. You will only need to prepare a small potful, as it is exceedingly sweet. Only supplement your wild petals with those from garden roses if it is absolutely necessary to make up the quantity: the thick, fleshy petals of the garden varieties are very difficult to reduce to jelly.

To make rose-petal jam, take two cups of wild rose petals. Sort through the petals, and remove any withered ones (cram them down into the cup when measuring). Dissolve two cups of castor sugar in half a cup of water, mixed with one tablespoon each of lemon juice and orange juice. Stir in the rose petals and put the pan over a very low heat. Stir continuously for half an hour, or until all the petals have 'melted'. Cool the mixture a little, pour into a small glass jar and seal.

DESCRIPTION
A slender shrub, with usually unbranched, arching stems growing up to 2m (6ft) high, and only very slightly spiny.

LEAVES
toothed and oval, and often whitish below.

FLOWERS
small and white in drooping clusters.

FRUIT
a rich red berry, formed by a number of drupelets, July–September.

HABITAT
widespread throughout the British Isles, and quite frequent in hedgerows, rocky woods, and heaths.

Raspberry
Rubus idacus

Although many raspberry plants growing in the wild are bird-seeded from cultivated stock, the fruit is as authentic a British native as its close relative the blackberry. It is not difficult to see why, of the two, it was the raspberry that was taken into gardens. It grows more tidily and with greater restraint than the spiny, aggressive bramble. And this of course means that it has been less prolific in the wild – another good reason for nurturing the plant in the non-competitive security of the garden. The berry is probably the best of all the soft fruits. Wordsworth, whose verse 'Foresight' is believed to be about the raspberry, clearly felt for it, and gave good picking advice if rather mediocre poetry:

> Hither soon as spring is fled
> You and Charles and I will walk;
> Lurking berries, ripe and red,
> Then will hang from every stalk,
> Each within its leafy bower;
> And for that promise spare the flower!

And 'as soon as spring is fled' is precisely when you will find it. It is usually the first soft fruit to ripen, occasionally as early as the last weeks of June. If you have difficulty distinguishing young raspberries from unripe blackberries, look at the stems on which they are growing. The raspberry has woody, cane-like stems, comparatively smooth except for a few weak prickles; the blackberry has much coarser stems armed with a great number of strong prickles.

The berries themselves are quite different in texture, even when they are similarly coloured. Raspberries have a matt, spongy surface, whilst blackberries are covered with a shiny, taut skin. And when fully ripe the raspberry comes away very easily from its pithy core.

Raspberries are such a rich and substantial fruit that it would be a waste to make jelly from them. But simmered in their own juice for about a quarter of an hour, and then boiled to setting point with an equal weight of sugar, they make a very fine jam.

If you only find a handful of wild berries, use them for stuffing game

birds, or to make the famous summer pudding. This needs no cooking, but must be made the day before it is needed. Cut some fairly thick slices of bread and remove the crusts. Moisten them with milk, and line the sides and bottom of a deep pudding basin with them. Make sure that the slices overlap well, so that they will hold together when turned out. Then fill the pudding basin with a mixture of cooked raspberries, and any red, white or black currants that are available. Cover the top with more slices of moistened bread, and then with greaseproof paper. Put a weight on top of the paper and leave the pudding to stand in the refrigerator overnight. Turn out of the mould carefully and serve with cream.

Raspberry vinegar

Sharp and thickish, raspberry vinegars have an ancient pedigree as sauces for fruit dishes and bases for summer drinks. Now they have a role in nouvelle cuisine, as ingredients in salad dressings and sauces for meat.

400g (16oz) raspberries

500ml (1 pint) white wine vinegar

1 Put 200g (8oz) of the raspberries in a bowl and cover with the white wine vinegar. Cover with a cloth and leave in a cool place for two or three days.

2 Strain, keeping the already red-tinged vinegar, and add another 200g (8oz) of raspberries and again keep for two or three days.

3 Strain, and decant the vinegar into a bottle which already contains a few more ripe raspberries. Close tightly.

Wild Strawberry

Fragaria vesca

DESCRIPTION
A low, creeping plant with hairy runners and stems 5–30cm (2–12in).

LEAVES
in groups of three, toothed, shiny green above and silky grey beneath.

FLOWERS
white and five-petalled.

FRUIT
small drooping red berries with seeds protruding, late June–September.

HABITAT
widespread and frequent on grassy banks, heaths, open woods, throughout Europe.

Wild strawberries prefer chalky soils, and in some places they can be found creeping over bare limestone rocks of exposed banks. These carry the best fruits of all, as they will have been warmed by the sun reflected from the rock, and their fragrance can be savoured to the full.

The plants can also grow in great numbers in newly cleared woods Gilbert White wrote of 'strawberry slidders' where the wood had been cut and hauled down Hampshire's hanging beechwoods. But here the fruit is less abundant and smaller, and it may take some time to gather a cup or two. Always look under the leaves as well as on top of the plant when picking wild strawberries. And to save bruising the fruit in a jar or basket, try the Swedish practice of threading them onto a long grass stalk.

What the wild strawberry lacks in size it more than makes up for in flavour. The ripe fruits are wonderfully concentrated beads of sweetness, which our ancestors appreciated in much the same way as we do. The most useful recipes are those which make the best of small quantities of berries. Try a wineglassful topped with champagne. Add a few to a fresh fruit salad – or a green salad, for that matter. Make use of their winey aroma by turning them into a sauce for other fruit (raspberries or peaches especially). Simply purée them with a little wine, pepper and sugar.

The strawberry has many medicinal properties; Linnaeus identified the berries as a cure for rheumatic gout; the root and leaves are a treatment for dysentry; and the juice can whiten teeth and relieve sunburn.

DESCRIPTION
A hairy, silvery, creeping
perennial
10–30cm(4–12in).

LEAVES
a basal rosette, coarsely
toothed.

FLOWERS
yellow, 5-petalled,
May–September.

HABITAT
an abundant flower of
damp grassy and waste
places.

Silverweed
Potentilla anserina

The undersides of the leaves are flashed with a pale matt grey, making the plant look withered before its time. Yet the tops are a silky, liquid green, and the leaves were once used by foot soldiers as an apparently cooling lining for their boots. The whole plant has a history of medicinal and culinary use going back to the Greeks.

The roots were cultivated as a crop from late prehistoric times. In the upland areas of Great Britain they were used right up until the introduction

of the potato – and later, in times of famine. The roots were boiled or baked or even eaten raw, and the botanist John Ray likened their taste to parsnip. They were also dried and ground into flour for bread and gruel.

Silverweed is worth bringing into your garden for its ambivalent leaves and yellow, utilitarian flowers. If you do, some of those old famine recipes for the roots are worth reviving.

DESCRIPTION
Short, erect, hairless
perennial with winged
stems, up to 40cm
(16in).

LEAVES
4–6 pairs of leaflets.

FLOWERS
2–16 purple-red flowers,
fading to blue,
April–July.

HABITAT
damp grassland and open
woods.

Bitter Vetch

Lathyrus montanus

Another edible tuber from the pea family. Bitter vetch is one of the commoner species, and sometimes grows in abundance in healthy areas. It has been recognised as a vegetable since at least the Middle Ages, and Gerard, later likening the taste of the roots to chestnut, has some typically muted praise for it:

> *'The Nuts of this Pease being boiled and eaten, are hardlier digested then be either Turneps or Parsneps, yet they do nourish no less then the Parsneps: they are not so windie as they, they do more slowly passe thorowe the belly by reason of their binding qualitie, and being eaten rawe, they be yet harder of digestion, and do hardlier and slowlier descend.'*

In later times the roots have been used as a subsistence crop in the Scottish Islands, either raw or dried. They have also been used for flavouring whisky.

Rest Harrow
Ononis repens

DESCRIPTION
Hairy, sticky, spreading perennial, 10–70cm (4–28in).

LEAVES
1 or 3 leaflets, oval, toothed.

FLOWERS
pink-purple, loose clusters, June–September.

HABITAT
grassland, shingle beaches, sand-dunes, lime-rich soil.

A common enough plant in dry and chalky grassland, but too handsome to pick needlessly. It is like a sweet pea bred for the rockery: short, pert and bushy. The root is tough and serpentine. In the north, children would dig it up and chew it; hence it acquired the names wild liquorice and Spanish root.

Marsh Mallow
Althaea officinalis

DESCRIPTION
A tall perennial 1.5–2m (5–6½ft), which grows in softly-branched clumps.

LEAVES
lobed, long-stalked.

FLOWERS
velvety-pink, July–September.

HABITAT
near salt water, on or near coastal areas

The plant that gave the sweet its name. Today marshmallow is made from starch, gelatine and sugar. But once it was produced from the roots of *Althaea officinalis*, which contain not only their own starch, but albumen, a crystallisable sugar, a fixed oil and a good deal of gelatinous matter. They were gathered by fishermen's wives in the dykes and saltmarshes of the East Coast, where the plant still grows. Also used in making cough syrup.

DESCRIPTION
Erect shrub up to 1.5m
(5ft) high.

LEAVES
hairless or downy
beneath, not aromatic.

FLOWERS
drooping, stalked spikes,
April–May.

FRUIT
translucent red berry.

HABITAT
damp woodland, hedges,
often by water.

Redcurrant
Ribes rubrum

The fruits of wild redcurrant are rarely copious enough to warrant cooking with, but they can make a bracing wayside nibble in high summer, in that pleasurable activity which the writer Edward Bunyard called 'ambulant consumption'. Look out for them in ancient woodland, by stream banks and in rough fens – though individuals naturalised from gardens can crop up anywhere.

The fruits appear from July, and are round and shiny, and often much less red than their cultivated cousins. (But avoid confusion with the cloying fruit of guelder rose. This is also a shrub of woods and riversides, but its berries lack a 'tail', and look heavy and waxy beside the almost translucent skins of the redcurrant.)

Blackcurrant

Ribes nigrum

DESCRIPTION
Erect shrub up to 1.5m
(5ft) high.

LEAVES
aromatic when crushed.

FLOWERS
drooping, stalked spikes,
April–May.

FRUIT
opaque black berry.

HABITAT
damp woodland, hedges,
often by water.

The soothing properties of blackcurrant juice were probably known long before the plant passed into cultivation, for it was often given against sore throats and 'the quinsy'. It is an uncommon plant in the wild, and can readily be told from redcurrant by its larger, heavily aromatic leaves. A few of these, dried, can transform a pot of Indian tea.

The currants can also be dried, and in this form they are one of the bases of pemmican, an Amerindian dish taken up by Polar explorers. The currants are pounded together with dried meat, and the mixture bound together and coated with fat or tallow. The result was a food containing almost all the ingredients necessary for a balanced diet, which would keep well even on long journeys.

Gooseberry

Ribes uva-crispa

DESCRIPTION
A low, many-branched
spiny shrub, 1.2m (4ft).

LEAVES
3- or 4-lobed blunt-
toothed.

FLOWERS
drooping red-tinged,
greens.

FRUIT
greenish-yellow, egg-
shaped and usually hairy,
from July.

HABITAT
widespread but scattered
in woods and hedgerows,
in most of Europe.

There is a widespread belief that wild gooseberries are all naturalised from
bird-sown garden varieties, and undoubtedly some wild specimens began
life this way. But the species is almost certainly native, especially in old
woods and on calcareous soils, and the traffic has been just as active the
other way, from the wild into cultivation. The history of the gooseberry's
domestication from lowly hedgerow berry to luscious dessert fruit is one of
the most extraordinary stories of vernacular plant breeding. Cultivated
gooseberries were not known until late in the 16th Century; yet by the end
of the 19th there were as many as 2,000 named varieties. The improvement
was due almost entirely to the ingenuity of amateur growers, especially in
the industrial Midlands, who were spurred on in their breeding programmes
by annual competitions (still held in a few villages).

You will find wild gooseberries from early July onwards, and on some

bushes (preferably with the assistance of gloves because of the spines you may be able pick a fair quantity, though they are very irregular fruiters. Depending on their size, ripeness and sweetness, you can use the berries in any of the recipes which normally employ the cultivated fruit. They can go into gooseberry pie or gooseberry fool, of if less ripe, into a gooseberry jelly.

Oldbury tarts, from Oldbury-on-Severn, were traditionally made with wild gooseberries and sold at Whitsuntide fairs (though the berries can hardly have been ripe at this time, and preserved fruit must have been used). The tarts were actually small pies, tea-cup sized, filled with gooseberries and demerera sugar.

An impromptu recipe, and one which can be used with a small quantity of berries, is for a fennel and gooseberry sauce for mackerel. Stew a handful of fruit in a little cider, pulp through a sieve, then mix with chopped fennel. Add mustard and honey to taste.

Gooseberry fool

I cup of wild gooseberries
½ cup of double cream
2 glasses of white wine
I tablespoon of honey
Wild rose petals to garnish

1 Top and tail the gooseberries. Stew in the white wine and honey, and reduce until the mixture is the consistency of jam.

2 Whip the cream until stiff

3 When the gooseberry mixture is cool, fold in the whipped cream.

4 Decorate with rose petals.

Common Mallow
Malva sylvestris

DESCRIPTION
A coarse, bushy, often
straggly plant, 20–100cm
(8–40in).

LEAVES
crinkly, ivy-shaped,
slightly clammy to touch
when young.

FLOWERS
5-petalled purplish
blossoms, up to 4cm
(2in) across
June–October.

HABITAT
widespread and abundant
on roadsides, banks and
waste places, throughout
Europe.

Mallow blooms late into the autumn, and its flowers have a strange, artificial elegance that is unexpected in such an obviously hardy wayside weed. The mauve petals are arched like some porcelain decoration, and veined with deep purple streaks.

The leaves stay green and fresh almost all the year, but are best picked in the summer months, when they are pale and stretch like films of gelatine. Always wash your leaves well and discard any that have developed a brownish rust, or are embedded with tiny black insect eggs.

Mallow leaves can be cooked as a spinach, but they are extremely glutinous, and a more attractive way of using them is to make them into soup. In Arab countries the leaves of related species are the basis of the famous soup, melokhia:

Melokhia is one of Egypt's national dishes. It is an ancient peasant soup, the making of which is believed to be portrayed in pharaonic tomb paintings. The medieval melokhia seems to have been a little richer, incorporating fried minced meat and chicken balls. Today, only a few families add these ... Peasant women prepare this soup almost daily. Protein stock is too expensive, so they cook the leaves in water in which a few vegetables have been boiled. The leaves give the soup a glutinous texture. The women cook the soup in large pots, which they carry to the fields on their heads for the men to eat at midday. When the work is done and the men come home, they eat it again at dusk with equal pleasure. Melokhia has recently acquired a symbolic and patriotic importance in Egypt, for it represents the national, popular taste as opposed to the more snobbish and cosmopolitan taste of the old regime. Most families have their own special way of preparing it, and the proportions vary according to the financial means, position and preferences of the people who make it.

from *Middle Eastern Food*, by Claudia Roden

ABOVE
Common mallow on
Chesil Beach, Dorset

To make a version of melokhia take about a pound of young mallow leaves, cut off the stalks, wash well, and chop very small or purée in a blender. Boil in about two pints of chicken stock for ten minutes. Then prepare a garlic sauce by frying two crushed cloves of garlic in a little oil until golden brown, adding a dessert-spoonful of ground coriander, a pinch of cayenne pepper, and some salt, and mixing to a paste in the hot pan. Add this paste to the soup, cover the saucepan tightly and simmer for two or three minutes, stirring occasionally to prevent the leaves falling to the bottom.

The melokhia can then be served on its own, or with boiled rice, or pieces of cooked meat and vegetables.

Common mallow is also known for its small, round seeds, called 'cheeses' (from their shape, rather than their taste, which is mildly nutty). Children in country districts still pick and eat these, though they're such a diminutive mouthful that their taste and texture are barely noticeable.

DESCRIPTION
Untidy perennial with grooved stems, 30–120cm (12–47in).

LEAVES
lobed leaves form a basal rosette.

FLOWERS
pale blue, June–September.

HABITAT
widespread throughout England and Wales, but locally common, usually on chalk soils in grassy and waste places.

RIGHT
Chicory, *Cichorium intybus*

FAR RIGHT
Goatsbeard, *Tragopogon pratensis*

Chicory
Cichorium intybus

The 'succory' of the old herbalists, a tall, distinguished plant with startling cornflower-blue blossoms. Chicory is probably not a native of the British Isles, but it still grows in quite a wide range of grassy habitats, especially on chalk and limestone.

The roots are boiled and eaten by the Arabs, and it is from the Arabic Chicouryeb that the English name for the plant is derived. Roast and ground, the roots make slightly bitter substitute for, or addition to, coffee, and have been extensively cultivated for this purpose. It was used on a wide scale during the Second World War when coffee supplies were cut off.

The leaves of chicory have been used as a salad vegetable in summer, as have the leaves of a number of other members of the daisy family. such as:

Nipplewort, *Lapsana communis*, widespread on shady banks, roadsides, etc.

Catsear, *Hypochoeris radicata*, common in pastures and other grassy places. In flower May–September, but the leaves grow through much of the winter.

Rough hawkbit, *Leontodon hispidus*, common in meadows, roadside verges, and dry grassy places.

Goatsbeard, *Tragopogon pratensis*, widespread in dry grassy places.

Wall lettuce, *Mycelis muralis*, widespread but rather local on rocks, walls and shady banks.

Perennial sow-thistle, *Sonchus arvensis*, prickly sow-thistle, *S. asper*. Widespread on road verges and cultivated ground.

Opinions are divided about the virtues of these plants. Pliny has Theseus dining off a dish of sow-thistles before going to finish off the

BELOW LEFT
Nipplewort,
Lapsana communis

BELOW MIDDLE
Catsear,
Hypochoeris radicata

BELOW RIGHT
Rough hawkbit,
Leontodon hispidus

Minotaur. Later writers often use the vernacular name 'hare's lettuce', and describe how the hare, 'when fainting with the heat, she recruits her strength with this herb'. John Ray, usually the enthusiastic one, simply dismisses it. 'We leave it to be masticated by hare's and rabbits'. For me they are amongst the best of these members of the daisy family, fleshier and milder than the dandelion. But you must trim off the bristles at the edge of the leaves before use.

DESCRIPTION
Robust perennial up to
1m (3ft) tall.

LEAVES
lower leaves long, up to
30cm (12in).

FLOWERS
a white cluster,
June–August.

HABITAT
near salt water;
saltmarshes, sand-dunes.

Dittander
Lepidium latifolium

Dittander has a hot, pungent root, and was gathered from the wild and occasionally grown in gardens as a condiment before horseradish and pepper became available and increasingly popular. It is a perennial and has an obstinate and aggressive root system like horseradish, yet is now uncommon in the wild. Only beside a few estuaries on the south and east coasts can the elegant and robust spires be found.

DESCRIPTION
Hairless biennial.

LEAVES
shiny, bright-green.

FLOWERS
yellowish,
June–September.

HABITAT
sandy and rocky banks,

Parsley
Petroselinum crispum

Garden parsley is a native of the Mediterranean, but is occasionally naturalised, especially on sandy and rocky banks near the sea. As a change from garnishing, try frying parsley for half a minute in hot butter, and serving it as a vegetable with fish.

Wild Asparagus
Asparagus officinalis

DESCRIPTION
Medium-tall branched perennial reaching to 2m (6½ft); young basal shoots 5–10mm thick.

LEAVES
short, needle-like tufts.

FLOWERS
bell-shaped, greenish-white, May–August.

FRUIT
red berry.

HABITAT
roadsides and waste ground.

RIGHT
Asparagus officinalis
ssp *prostratus*

Several species of wild asparagus grow in Europe, especially in scrub in the Mediterranean region, and in the south are probably the most popular wild vegetable of all. In Britain a prostrate sub-species occurs occasionally on the coast in the South-west, and naturalised specimens of the cultivated ssp *officinalis* appear on roadsides and waste ground almost anywhere.

Around the Mediterranean, the young shoots or spears, with their characteristic scaly, snake's-head tips, can be found winding their way through hedges and rough ground from March onwards. Pick the shoots 20–30cm (8–12in) long and cook briefly as you would cultivated asparagus. A popular way of serving them is with eggs, as in an Italian frittata (see p.15) or a Spanish huelvos, in which the chopped asparagus is briefly stir-fried, and then stirred into scrambled eggs.

DESCRIPTION
Short hairless annual
with a solid stem.

LEAVES
opposite, lobed.

FLOWERS
white or pink; outer
flowers with large outer
petals, June–August.

FRUIT
red-brown, ridged,
aromatic when crushed.

HABITAT
occasionally naturalised
on waste ground.

Coriander
Coriandrum sativum

Coriander is a native of the eastern and southern Mediterranean, and is occasionally naturalised in waste places in Britain. The flavour of the green leaves is strong and slightly soapy, and they are popular additions to Mediterranean salads and stews. The dried seeds are mentioned in Exodus and are one of the oldest spices known to man. Ground up, they are an essential ingredient of most curries and will add a subtle flavour to soups and, above all, pork dishes. Len Deighton's recommendation: 'hurl crushed coriander seeds into any open pot you see.'

Pignut
Conopodium majus

DESCRIPTION
Slender, single-stemmed
perennial, 20–80cm
(8–32in).

LEAVES
feathery with narrow
lobes.

FLOWERS
white, in dense, flat
heads, May–July. Fruit:
ridged, egg-shaped.

HABITAT
on well-drained soils in
grassland and woodland.

Digging up pignuts is now illegal, except with the landowner's permission. Once, they were one of the most popular wild foods amongst children, even though extracting them from the ground was as delicate a business as an egg and spoon race. They cannot be pulled out, for the thin leaf stalk breaks off very quickly. The fine white roots must be unearthed with a knife and carefully traced down to the tuber, which lies about 10–20cm (4–8in) below the surface.

The roundish 'nuts', dark brown and the size of walnuts, can be eaten raw, and taste somewhere between hazel nuts and celery. They were also often added to stews, when the taste reputedly becomes more like parsnip.

Pignuts are worth trying if you have legal access to the roots. They are still quite common on unimproved grassland and heath, and in open woods, and can be recognised by their fine, thready foliage.

DESCRIPTION
Aromatic, hairy,
branched perennial,
1–1.5m (4–5ft).

LEAVES
fine-cut, feathery,
aniseed-scented when
crushed.

FLOWERS
large white umbels,
May–July.

FRUIT
green, ribbed, 15–25mm
(up to 1in).

HABITAT
waysides, grasslands and
stream banks.

Sweet Cicely
Myrrhis odorata

Cicely is one of the few plants where the connotation 'sweet' refers as much to taste as to smell. The feathery leaves have distinctly sugary overtones to their mild aniseed flavour, and are ideal for flavouring stewed fruits such as gooseberries and plums.

The species was probably introduced to this country by the Romans, and in some places it is still known as the 'Roman plant'. It is now widely naturalised in northern Britain, and makes a handsome show on roadsides against a background of drystone walls. The 16th Century herbalist John Gerard was a great fan. He called the plant 'sweet chervil' and recommended both the roots (boiled) and the leaves in salads. However, he regarded the seeds as far and away the plant's choicest part:

'the seeds eaten as a sallad whilest they are yet greene, with oyle, vinegar and pepper, exceed all other sallads by many degrees, both in pleasantness of taste, sweetnesse of smell, and wholesomeness for the cold and feeble stomacke.'

His recommendation and recipe still hold good, yet there is no need to go to such trouble. The green seeds of cicely, which resemble miniature gherkins, are excellent off-the-bush nibbles. Their crisp texture and sweet-and-sour aniseed taste also make them an excellent foil to bread and cheese during a wayside picnic.

In France, the young leaves, blanched and deep-fried in a little light batter, are served as an hors d'oeuvre.

The uses of this plant are not confined to the kitchen. It is one of the herbs used in the making of Chartreuse, and in Westmoreland the leaves were used to polish oak panels.

DESCRIPTION
A thistle-like, spiny,
blue-green perennial,
20–60cm (8–24in).

LEAVES
three-lobed, spiny with
pale veins and margins.

FLOWERS
blue, in rounded heads
with spiny bracts,
June–August.

FRUIT
egg-shaped.

HABITAT
locally common on sandy
and shingle beaches.

Sea Holly

Eryngium maritimum

A beautiful plant of the seashore which has suffered much for the sake of holidaymakers' vases. It is a thistle-like plant, its spiny, ice-blue leaves covered with bloom and ribbed and edged with a fine white tracery of veins. It likes the rough ground of sandy and shingly beaches, and its roots have consequently been confused more than once with those of the vitriolic horned poppy, with curious results:

> *'a certain person made a pye of the roots of this plant,*
> *supposing them to be the roots of the Eryngo, of which he had*
> *before eaten pyes which were very pleasant, and eating it while*
> *it was hot, became delirious, and having voided a stool in a*
> *white chamber pot, fancied it to be gold, breaking the pot in*
> *pieces, and desiring what he imagined as gold might be*
> *preserved as such. Also his man and maid servant eating of the*
> *same pye, fancied of what they saw to be gold.'*

Philosophical Transactions, 1698 quoted in *The Englishman's Flora*

Sea holly roots, as Eryngo roots, were once extensively used for making candied sweetmeats. The roots were dug up (they could be up to 2m (6ft)

long in the spring or autumn), partly boiled until they could be peeled and then cut into thin slices. These were cooked with an equal weight of sugar until the latter became syrup, when the roots were removed and allowed to cool. Candied Eryngo roots were a vital ingredient of that redoubtable Elizabethan dish, marrow-bone pie.

DESCRIPTION
An evergreen shrub, up
to 1m (3ft) tall.

LEAVES
numerous, tiny in
opposite rows.

FLOWERS
purple and bell-shaped
and carried in spikes,
August–September.

HABITAT
widespread and often
abundant on heaths,
moors and open woods
on acid soils, throughout
north-western Europe.

RIGHT
Ling and lichens,
Lakenheath Warren,
Suffolk

Heather

Calluna vulgaris

Heather of ling is the dominant plant over much of western Europe's upland moors and sandy wastes. In full flower – lilac billows as far as the eye can see – a heather moor is a glorious sight. But it is also a deceptive one, for sweeps of ling are signs of a depleted soil and a harsh climate. It flourishes in conditions that arable crops would find intolerable, and in acid ground that has been cleared of its trees.

For those who share its impoverished habitats, it has been an absolute necessity of domestic life, a stand-in for a whole range of absent plants. It has been used as the foundation for wattle-and-daub walls, to thatch roofs, sweep floors and fuel ovens. Its fibrous stems have been woven into ropes, and its roots carved into knife handles (particularly for ceremonial Scottish dirks). Its flowering tops make an orange dye. Sheep and grouse thrive on the shoots, too (which is just as well, as heather moors are often the result of drastic forest clearances carried out for the benefit of these animals).

And it will be no surprise to any walker who has rested in the heather that it was also universally used as bedding, for man and beast alike. It is so soft, supporting and fragrant that Scottish settlers took it to America with them, and naturalised it in a continent thousands of miles outside its natural range.

Heather has also been used in the kitchen. Its flowers are so rich in nectar that beekeepers often transport their hives many miles to a stretch of health or moorland when the heather is in bloom, and most of the recipes for heather make use of this honey-rich blossom. A famous, if complicated use, is in the making of heather ale. This has recently been revived commercially by the Glasgow brewer Bruce Williams, according to a Pictish recipe, and sold under the name of Freoch. It is wonderfully fragrant with the scents of heather and honey.

The dried flower heads make a good tea, and Robert Burns is supposed to have drunk a moorland tea based on heather tops mixed with the dried leaves of bilberry, blackberry, speedwell, thyme and wild strawberry.

DESCRIPTION
A shrub with hairless
twigs, growing 20–50cm
(8–20in) high.

LEAVES
oval, slightly toothed.

FLOWERS
solitary, drooping,
greenish-pink globes,
April–June.

FRUITS
small, round, black and
covered with bloom, July
to September.

HABITAT
widespread and locally
abundant on heaths and
moors, and as the
understorey in conifer
woods in northern
Europe.

Bilberry, Whortleberry

Vaccinium myrtillus

Bilberries transport you more thoroughly into the role of the hunter-gatherer than perhaps any other wild food. The fruit, for a start, is virtually unknown in cultivation – a source of continual bafflement to anyone who has sampled the succulent, winey berries. (The blueberries bought from greengrocers are a larger and less flavoursome American species.) Then there is the bilberry's favoured habitat, on windswept moors and acid woods in the uplands. Finally, because they crop low down, the collector will be forced to do most of the picking on all fours, chimpanzee-style.

Yet the picking is a large part of the fun. In some parts of mainland Europe bilberry gathering has been partially mechanised with the help of a combined comb and shovel known as a 'peigne.' This device, as well as damaging the more fragile shoots and stripping many of the leaves as well as the berries, robs the picker of the pleasure of hunting for clusters of fruit under the leaves, and one's fingers (and mouth!) turning blue.

In Britain the wild fruit is still picked commercially on a small scale, particularly in the Welsh border country. The berries are sold in markets and to local pubs. Bilberries can be used to make jams, jellies, stews and cheesecakes. They can be frozen, or left to stand in the sun for a week or so, by which time they will have dried sufficiently to keep over the winter.

Some of the most interesting recipes come from Yorkshire. Bilberry pies are known in the area as 'mucky-mouth pies' because of the colour they give to tongues and lips, and are served at funeral teas. A few springs of mint are sometimes added to the fruit before cooking.

Bilberry pudding

A classic northern recipe, which sets the fruit in a kind of Yorkshire pudding.

4 tbsp flour

I egg

I large cup of milk

2 tbsp of brown sugar

200g (8oz) approx. of bilberries

1 Make a thinnish batter by beating the egg with the sugar and then slowly adding the milk.

2 Stir in the sugar and the bilberries.

3 Pour into a greased tin

4 Bake in a medium oven for half an hour.

Cranberry

Vaccinium oxycoccus

DESCRIPTION
Creeping, evergreen dwarf shrub, 50cm (20in).

LEAVES
dark-green, pointed, whitish beneath.

FLOWER
pink with down-turned petals, June–August.

FRUIT
round, mottled red.

HABITAT
bogs, marshy heaths.

Cranberries were once more common in Britain. But the draining of much of our marsh and upland bog has robbed the species of its native habitat, and it is now largely confined to the peatlands in the north of England and Wales.

The berry is mottled red and less than 1cm (½in) across, and is carried on a creeping shrub. It is more or less inedible raw, but can be made into sauces and jellies, just like its larger American relatives, which is famous for making a sauce for turkey. In fact cranberry recipes were taken to America by British settlers and transferred to the indigenous species.

Crowberry
Empetrum nigrum

DESCRIPTION
A small creeping shrub, 30cm (12in).

LEAVES
linear, edges rolled under.

FLOWERS
small, pink, April–June.

FRUIT
shiny black when ripe.

HABITAT
bogs, moors.

The fruits are used in Arctic regions and have some value as a source of Vitamin C. Although the berries are difficult to gather in any quantity, some collectors have enjoyed a jelly made from them. In Britain the crowberry is found trailing over some northern moorland.

Cowberry, Lingonberry
Vaccinium vitis-idaea

DESCRIPTION
Small, evergreen shrub, 40cm (16in).

LEAVES
leathery, oval, untoothed.

FLOWER
pink or white, open in clusters, May–July.

FRUIT
red, spherical.

HABITAT
moorland, bogs.

A low evergreen bush growing on depleted peatland soils in northern Europe. The red spherical berries are sharp and are usually made into jam or jelly (though they need added pectin). Like cloudberry (*Rubus chamaemorus*) they contain a natural preservative, a derivative of benzoic acid, which means that they can be stored quite successfully. They are popular in Sweden, where they are known as 'the red gold of the forests'.

DESCRIPTION
Hairy perennial,
10–120cm (4–47in).

LEAVES
narrow, pointed.

FLOWERS
yellow, scented in dense
clusters.

HABITAT
sand-dunes, dry-
grasslands, shingle
beaches.

Lady's Bedstraw
Galium verum

A feathery plant of meadows and heathland, whose yellow flowers smell of honey when fresh. When the plant is dried it develops the characteristic hay-like smell of coumarin, (like sweet woodruff, also a member of the bedstraw family). This breaks down to yield a powerful anti-coagulant, dicoumarol. Yet lady's bedstraw also contains some chemical with contrary properties, since it is of proven value as a styptic. It was also once used as a kind of vegetable rennet, for curdling milk into junkets and cheese, though details of the process have not survived.

DESCRIPTION
A hairless perennial with
trailing, reddish stems up
to 60 cm (24in) high.

LEAVES
fleshy, blue-green.

FLOWERS
in clusters, pink turning
blue, June–August.

HABITAT
shingle beaches on
coasts.

Oyster Plant
Mertensia maritimum

Oyster plant grows on a few stretches of coastal shingle in Scotland, in prostrate mats. The fleshy leaves have been eaten both raw and cooked, and taste like oysters. The similarity is close enough to have caused pseudo-shellfish poisoning in a person allergic to oysters!

DESCRIPTION
A loosely bushy annual,
with conspicuously hairy
stems, 30–60cm
(12–24in).

LEAVES
hairy with wavy edges.

FLOWERS
bright blue, with reflexed
petals and prominent
purple stamens,
May–September.

HABITAT
quite common as an
escape on waysides and
waste places.

Borage
Borago officinalis

Borage once had a great reputation as a sort of herbal pep-pill. It was renowned as an aphrodisiac and as a general dispeller of melancholy and depression. John Evelyn clearly understood the type of person who would perennially be in need of such aids when he wrote that 'the sprigs ... are of known virtue to revive the hypochondriac and cheer the hard student'.

Whatever its medicinal qualities, the young leaves and bright blue, star-like flowers make a refreshing and fragrant addition to claret cups and other summer drinks, particularly in combination with woodruff. The star-shaped petals look appealing floated out on top of the drink – or frozen inside ice cubes. In more leisurely days, Richard Jeffries noted in *Nature Near London* (1883), borage leaves used 'to float in the claret cup ladelled out to thirsty travellers at the London railway stations'.

DESCRIPTION
A rough, hairy mint,
often growing in quite
sizeable clumps up to
60cm (2ft) high.

LEAVES
frequently tinged with
purple, and grow in
opposed pairs.

FLOWERS
bluish-lilac, growing in a
round bushy head at the
top of the plant,
July–September.

HABITAT
widespread and common
by the edges of streams,
in damp meadows, and
woods, throughout the
British Isles.

Water Mint
Mentha aquatica

This, our commonest waterside mint, has a flavour reminiscent of peppermint (*Mentha piperita* which is in fact a cross between this variety and spearmint, *M. spicata*). It often grows quite abundantly near water, its leaves immensely varied in size and coloration, but always crowned with a fine bush of lilac flowers.

It is cleaner and more piercing in smell and flavour than corn mint (M. arvensis), and better as an addition to cooked dishes. John Gerard was a great fan: 'The savour or smell of the water mint rejoiceth the hart of man'. What better way to make use of this than that cool transatlantic drink, Mint Julep? Wash a bunch of mint, put it in a basin and bruise it with the back of a spoon. Add one cup of sugar, one tin of pineapple juice and the juice of four lemons. Stir the mixture well and allow to stand for about four or five hours. Strain into a jug, and add three bottles of dry ginger ale, ice cubes, some thin slices of lemon and a very few sprigs of fresh mint. (The Americans also add a good slug of Bourbon for an extra kick!)

There are so many well-known uses for the more aromatic mints in cooking, that I cannot resist the temptation to give here the recipe for a real mint folly: mint and marshmallow custard (see right).

If you cannot face this, try adding mint to your cooked egg and cheese dishes as well as to the peas and spuds. Alternatively, use water mint leaves to make mint tea, steeping the leaves in hot (not boiling water for about five minutes.

There are over a dozen varieties of mint growing wild in the British Isles, most of them quite rare. The following are the most interesting in culinary terms. All of them can be used for cooking, especially apple (M. rotundifolia) and spearmint (M. spicata), both commonly naturalised on roadsides in ditches and waste places.

These are a couple of the descriptions the 18th Century botanist William Sole gave of their savours in his classic *Menthae Britannicae*: Corn mint, M. *arvensis*

'has a strong fullsome mixed smell of mellow apples and gingerbread'.

Sole's spotting of the hint of gingerbread was perceptive, as corn mint is almost certainly an ancestor of the yellow-striped garden variety known as 'ginger mint'. His 'strong-scented mint' (which may be our sharp-toothed mint M. *x villosonervata* 'has a very strong volatile mixed smell of volatile salt and amber, camphor and mint' and is 'an honourable relict of our venerable Gothick ruins'. Sole's simile for the scent of water mint, incidentally was

'*exactly that of a ropy chimney in a wet summer, where wood fires have been kept in winter-time*'.

LEFT ABOVE
Water mint, *Mentha aquatica.*

LEFT BELOW
Corn mint, *Mentha arvensis.*

BELOW
Apple mint, *Mentha rotundifolia.*

RIGHT
Spearmint, *Mentha piperata.*

FAR RIGHT
Peppermint, *Mentha spicata.*

Mint and marshmallow custard

3 eggs
500ml (1 pint) milk
3 tsp chopped water mint
1 tbsp sugar
24 marshmallows

1 Beat together the eggs and sugar in a casserole and gradually stir in the milk.

2 Float on the surface the chopped water mint, and on top of this the 24 marshmallows.

3 Stand the dish in a shallow tray of water, and bake in a moderate over until set.

Marjoram
Origanum vulgare

DESCRIPTION
A slender herb, growing
up to 1m (3ft) with
downy stems extensively
branched near the top of
the plant.

LEAVES
oval, untoothed.

FLOWERS
pale, pinkish-purple
(sometimes white in
bunches at the head of
the plant), July–October.

HABITAT
widespread and common
in grassy places on
calcareous soils,
throughout Europe.

Wild marjoram, or oregano, is one of the elemental flavours of Mediterranean cooking. It belongs with that pervasive mixture of tomato and garlic and olive oil and adds a warm, earthy fragrance that seems to capture the essence of the hot south. In Britain, marjoram never achieves quite the rough fragrance it does in sunnier parts. However, gathered in summer it is perfect for drying, and used in winter it recalls something of the spirit of warmer months.

For use as a herb pick some sprigs of the plant, flowers and all, when it is just coming into bloom. The strip the leaves and blossoms from the rather wiry stalk. But be on the watch for discoloured or 'burnt' leaves. The plant is prone to moulds and rusts, and infected leaves, though harmless, are usually musty to taste.

Oregano goes especially well in stews and casseroles, in pasta sauces, and with Mediterranean vegetables. An interesting recipe is for olives oregano. When olives are steeped in a marinade of flavoured olive oil, they acquire something of the aroma of the herb. Simply steep the pricked olives in a cup of olive oil mixed with crushed peppercorns and plenty of chopped marjoram. Leave for two days, turning from time to time.

Another recipe involving the infusion of wild marjoram's aroma is a 16th Century German one for marjoram sugar. Add plenty of chopped flowers and buds and a few young leaves to a jar of caster sugar, and stand in the sun for a day. The scent will subtly transfer to the sugar, which can be used for sprinkling on cake, fruit and desserts.

In the south of England tea made from marjoram leaves used to be popular, and large quantities were gathered and hung up to dry.

Marjoram has been used for medical purposes since ancient times, either in infusions or as an oil. This was used to treat a variety of ailments such as convulsions, dropsy and poisoning. It was also used for pain relief, bringing out fevers in diseases such as measles and for treating stomach complaints such as colic.

Herb scones

50g (2oz) butter

100g (4oz) salted flour

1 heaped tsp chopped marjoram

1   Rub the butter into the flour until it resembles breadcrumbs

2   Add the marjoram, and enough cold water to make a stiff dough. Mix well but lightly with a knife, and then shape into flat cakes with your hands.

3   Put them on a greased tray in a hot oven for a 12–15 minutes or until risen.

4   Serve with roasted meat or vegetables

DESCRIPTION
A prostrate, tufted or
creeping plant, with
rather woody stems
and runners,
5–10cm (2–4in).

LEAVES
very small, oval and
ranged in many opposing
pairs along the stalks.

FLOWERS
pinkish purple in
rounded bunches at the
end of the stalks,
June–August.

HABITAT
widespread and often
common in grassy places,
especially on chalk and
limestone, and on sandy
heaths.

Wild Thyme

Thymus drucei

Wild thyme is one of the most pleasantly scented of herbs. But it is not often that you will find it sufficiently abundant or fragrant to fill your nostrils with that heady aroma as you are striding over the turf. British wild thymes are more retiring and less pungent than their garden relatives – and for that matter than the species that grow so conspicuously in the Mediterranean *maquis*. When it is not in flower finding it can be a hands-and-knees job, a rummage through the miniature downland flora, the milkworts and violets, for a sprig of tiny, oval leaves that yield that clovy smell between the fingers. Then, tracing the runners back, following their meanderings through the dry lower stems of the grasses back to the woody root.

For a short while, when each plant is in flower, picking is a simpler exercise – though less rewarding I think than the fingertip ferreting for the spring and autumn shoots. The flower heads are large compared to the size of the plant, and like marjoram conspicuous for their attendant insects. Wild thyme is best picked when in full bloom, so that the honey-scented flowers can be used as well as the leaves.

If you like you can strip the leaves and flowers off the stalk before

using. But as wild thyme is considerably milder than the garden variety you can afford to use large sprigs of it liberally – and indeed to try it out in unconventional combinations. The great virtue of wild thyme is precisely that versatility.

Try it as a tea, or chopped finely and beaten into butter. Add it to omelettes and to stuffings for roast chicken. But think of it, too, as a convenient way of perking up picnic or outdoor food. A few sprigs can be added to pots of cottage cheese, tucked inside sandwiches, thrown into almost any casserole and wrapped up with roast joints in foil. In Scandinavia, steeped in aquavit, it makes one of the favourite varieties of schnapps.

Thyme soup

A simple but comforting Catalan shepherd's recipe from Patience Gray's classic *Honey From A Weed*

1 bunch of dried wild thyme

Several slices of dry white bread

Olive oil

1 Soak the bread in olive oil

2 Infuse the thyme in boiling water for five minutes

3 Pour this over the oily bread and serve

Red Valerian
Centranthus ruber

DESCRIPTION
Blue-green, hairless perennial, 30–80cm (12–32in).

LEAVES
spear-shaped, in opposite pairs.

FLOWERS
red, sometimes pink or white, in branched clusters, May–September.

HABITAT
local on walls, old buildings, wasteland and cliffs.

In France and Italy the very young leaves of this plant are sometimes boiled with butter as greens, or eaten raw in salads – though they are rather bitter used this way.

Red valerian was introduced to Britain from Southern Europe in the 16th Century, and was a great favourite of Gerard's, though he ascribed no practical uses for the plant. Its clusters of red flowers now adorn many stony and rocky places in the South-west.

Common Chamomile, Lawn Chamomile

Chamaemelum nobile

DESCRIPTION
Hairy, spreading perennial.

LEAVES
feathery.

FLOWERS
daisy-like, June–September.

HABITAT
grassy and heathy places.

Common chamomile is not common at all; in fact it is a rather rare plant of grassy and heathy places in the south of England. It has a daisy-like flower and feathery leaves, but being a member of the huge and complex Compositae family this is scarcely enough to identify it. It can be told from the very similar scentless mayweed and corn chamomile by an absence of down beneath its leaves. But its most conspicuous characteristic is its sweet apple scent, for which it was once much valued in rockeries, and even planted on lawns instead of grass. Indeed, the name is derived from an ancient Greek word meaning 'ground apple'. The Greeks, Romans and Egyptians all believed it to have healing qualities.

Chamomile is still cultivated on a small scale for its flower-heads, which make a fine herbal tea. The heads are gathered when the petals just begin to turn down, and are used either fresh or dried. To dry the flowers, pick the opened heads carefully (using scissors) and spread on paper. Wait until the heads are papery and then store in a screw-top jar until needed.

Chanterelle
Cantharellus cibarius

DESCRIPTION
Egg-yolk yellow in colour
and smelling slightly of
apricots.

CAP
shaped like a funnel,
2.5–7.5cm (1–3 in)
across.

GILLS
like fan-vaulting or
veins, shallow, much-
forked and continuous
with the stem.

RING
none.

HABITAT
fairly common in all
kinds of woodland, but
especially beech,
July–December.

Chanterelles have long been regarded as among the most desirable fungi; an 18th-Century writer said that if they were placed in the moths of dead men they would come to life again. And in a list produced by Legg in 1990, the chanterelle was rated equal fourth together with wood blewitt, behind cep and parasol mushroom. In her book *Food of England*, Dorothy Hartley describes a search for them thus:

> *'You find them, suddenly, in the autumn woods, sometimes*
> *clustered so close that they look like a torn golden shawl*
> *dropped amongst the dead leaves and sticks.'*

Because they are not often infected by maggots or other insects, and are unlikely to be confused with any dangerous species, chanterelles ('girolles')

are extensively eaten throughout mainland Europe. They are slightly tougher than some other fungi and should be stewed slowly with milk for at least ten minutes. The result is delicately perfumed and slightly peppery. They can also be sliced and fried with garlic, parsley or lemon juice. Perhaps because of colour sympathy, chanterelles have always been associated with eggs, and there is scarcely any better way of serving previously-cooked specimens than in omelettes or with scrambled eggs.

Two fairly common relations of Chanterelle are Horn of Plenty, *Craterellus cornucopoides*, and Hedgehog fungus, *Hydnum repandum*, both used in much the same way.

Be careful of false chanterelle (*Hygrophoropsis aurantiaca*) which is not worth eating and may be poisonous to some. This species is more common with with conifers and on heathland. It is more orange than the true chanterelle, with a thin stem and lacks the fruity smell. Also avoid Jack O'Lantern (*Omphalotus olearius*) which occasionally appears on sweet chestnut and oak trees in southern England. It has an unpleasant smell. Finally there are two *Cortinarius* species (*C. orellanus* and *C. speciossimus*), both are rare but also poisonous.

DESCRIPTION
Large, up to 15cm (6in)
with white caps that
yellow with age; smells of
almonds. Resembles a
large Field Mushroom
(see pp.00).

CAP
up to 20cm (8in) across
when mature, bruises
yellow-brown on
handling.

GILLS
greyer than field
mushroom, free.

RING
double.

HABITAT
pastures, lawns,
July–November.

Horse Mushroom
Agaricus arvensis

A large fungus, sometimes as large as a plate, this close cousin of the field mushroom is also becoming uncommon. Sometimes avoided because of its tendency to bruise, it is meaty and flavouful, and if you only succeed in finding one mature specimen you have enough for a good meal. Remember to check for maggots. Avoid specimens that bruise bright yellow – this includes the poisonous yellow-staining mushroom.

If your specimens are still dome-shaped, they can be stuffed with whole tomatoes; if they are flat, grilled whole like steaks. An unusual recipe for either type is to stew them in milk, drain, set in a dish of white sauce, and then garnish with hot redcurrants. The dish is a contrast in colour and texture: the bright and sharp against the dark and fleshy. Otherwise use as field mushroom. Similar *Agaricus* spp. are *A. silvicola* and *A. macrosporus*.

DESCRIPTION
Similar to horse
mushroom, but smaller,
5–12cm (2–5in).

CAP
5–11cm (2–4in) across;
creamy-white often with
small grey-brown scales
in the middle.

GILLS
white at first, turning
grey-pink and finally
dark brown.

RING
down-turned.

HABITAT
grassland, parks and
gardens in summer and
autumn.

Yellow-staining Mushroom

Agaricus xanthodermus

Although not poisonous to everyone, if eaten the yellow-staining mushroom, *Agaricus xanthodermus* (see photograph above, and description left) can cause a nasty stomach upset. When collecting mushrooms if you are in any doubt then do not eat them.

BELOW
Agaricus macrosporus

AUTUMN

To bend with apples the moss'd cottage-trees,

And fill all fruit with ripeness to the core;

To swell the gourd, and plump the hazel shells

With a sweet kernel; to set budding more

To Autumn, John Keats 1795–1821

DESCRIPTION
An evergreen shrub
1.5–3.5m (4–12ft) high
(there is also a prostrate
form).

LEAVES
prickly needles in whorls
of three.

FLOWERS
small, yellow, at the base
of the leaves, May–June.

FRUIT
initially a green, berry-
like cone appearing in
June; ripens in
September or October of
its second year, when it
turns blue-black.

HABITAT
locally common on chalk
downs, limestone hills,
heaths and moors, chiefly
in south-east England
and the North.

Juniper
Juniperus communis

When they ripen, in September or October of their second year, blue-black juniper berries are rich in oil – the source of their use as a flavouring. They are probably best known for their association with gin, although home-grown berries have not been used by British distillers for over 100 years. By all means experiment with drinks in which the berries have been steeped. Even gin is improved by, as it were, a double dose.

Uses across Europe are varied: they have been roasted and ground as a coffee substitute. In Sweden they are used to make a type of beer, and are often turned into jam. In France, *genevrette* is made by fermenting a mixture of juniper berries and barley. Crushed berries are becoming increasingly popular as a flavouring for white meat dishes, particularly game.

Juniper berries are used to make a sauce for pork chops in Belgium. The chops are sealed on both sides and then placed in a shallow casserole. Sprinkle with lemon juice, and then add parsley, four crushed juniper berries, rosemary and salt and pepper. Arrange peeled and sliced apples over the top and then pour over melted butter. Cook in a medium oven for half an hour.

BELOW
Juniper and guelder rose
in autumn on chalk
downland, Noar Hill,
Hampshire

Walnut
Juglans regia

DESCRIPTION
Deciduous tree with a spreading crown and grey, fissured bark, up to 30m (100ft).

LEAVES
alternate, pinnate, with 5–9 leaflets.

FLOWERS
male catkins on new growth; female clusters on old wood.

FRUIT
green, fleshy 4–5cm (2in), the walnut is the wrinkled stone inside.

HABITAT
where cultivated, sometimes in woodland parks.

A native of southern Europe, the walnut has been cultivated in this country for some 500 years, for its wood and its fruit – the familiar walnut. Although not quick to spread outside cultivation, there some self-sown trees in warm spots such as hedgerows, and seeds can be carried away from parent trees by birds and mammals.

Walnuts are best when they are fairly ripe and dry, in late October and November. Before this the young 'wet' walnuts are rather tasteless. If you wish to pick them young, pick them in July whilst they are still green and make pickle from them. They should be soft enough to pass a knitting needle or skewer through. Prick them lightly with a fork to allow the pickle to permeate the skin, and leave them to stand in strong brine for about a week, until they are quite black. Drain and wash them and let them dry for 2–3 days more. Pack them into jars and cover them with hot pickling vinegar. Seal the jars and allow to stand for at least a month before eating.

Walnuts make a good cream sauce for mushroom cutlets. Process or chop the mushrooms finely, cook in a little butter and drain. Soak 125g (5oz) of soft breadcrumbs in milk and squeeze dry. Dice and sauté an onion, beat together two eggs and chop some parsley. Combine all the ingredients, form into cutlets and fry in oil. Finally, chop the walnuts and parsley and blend with cream and season.

Hazel

Corylus avellana

DESCRIPTION
Deciduous shrub,
1.5–3.5m (4–12ft)'
Leaves: roundish, downy
and toothed.

FLOWERS
male catkins yellow,
known as 'lamb's tails',
appear in the winter;
female small clusters.

FRUIT
1–2.5cm (½–1in) long,
ovoid and encased in a
green, leafy cup,
August–November.

HABITAT
abundant throughout the
British Isles except in
very damp areas. Grows
in woods, hedgerows and
scrubland.

A small, hardy tree, and more often a multi-stemmed shrub, the hazel was among the first species to recolonise the British Isles after the last Ice Age. An extremely useful tree, the leaves can be used as food for livestock, its branches for building fences and shelters, and of course its nuts can be eaten as food. Widely eaten in prehistoric times, the hazelnut even became part of Celtic legend – its compact shape, hard shell and nutritious fruit was an emblem of concentrated wisdom.

Try not to pick hazelnuts too early as they are likely to be soft and tasteless. They ripen in mid-September, at about the same time as the leaves begin to yellow, you may have to compete with the birds and squirrels, as the nuts do not just provide a tasty treat for us! Look for them at the edges of woods and in mature hedges. Search inside bushes for the nuts, as well as working round them, and scan them with the sun behind you if possible. Use a walking stick to bend down the branches, and gather

the nuts into a basket that stays open when you are picking: a plastic bag with one handle looped over your picking wrist is a useful device.

If the ground cover under the bush is relatively clear of grass, then it is worthwhile giving the bush a shake. Some of the invisible ripe nuts should find their way onto the ground after this. In fact it is always worth searching the ground underneath a hazel. If there are nuts there which are dark or grey-brown in colour then the kernels will have turned to dust. But there is a chance that there will also be fresh windfalls that have not yet been picked on by birds.

Once you have gathered your nuts, keep them in a dry, warm place – but in their shells, so that the kernels don't dry out as well. You can use the nuts chopped or grated in salads, or with apple, raisins and raw oatmeal (museli). Ground up in a blender, mixed with milk and chilled, they make a passable imitation of the Spanish drink 'horchata' (properly made from the roots of the sedge *Cyperus esculentus*). But hazelnuts are such a rich food that it seems wasteful not to use them occasionally as a protein substitute. Weight for weight they contain 50 per cent more protein, seven times more fat, and five times more carbohydrate than hen's eggs. An old-style vegetarian staple, the nut cutlet, makes maximum use of this protein source (see right).

Hazel leaves were used in the 15th Century to make a 'noteye', a highly-spiced pork stew. The leaves were ground together and mixed with ginger, saffron, sugar, salt and vinegar, before being added to minced pork.

Nut cutlet

50g (2oz) oil
50g (2oz) flour
500ml (1 pint) stock
75g (3oz) breadcrumbs
50g (2oz) grated hazelnuts
Milk or beaten egg for glazing
Salt and pepper

1 Mix the oil and the flour in a saucepan. Add the stock and stew for ten minutes, stirring all the time.

2 Add the breadcrumbs and grated hazelnuts. Season.

3 Cool the mixture and shape into cutlets.

4 Glaze the cutlets, coat with breadcrumbs, and fry in the oil until golden brown.

Beech
Fagus sylvatica

DESCRIPTION
A stately, deciduous tree,
with smooth, grey bark,
to 40m (130ft).

LEAVES
bright green, alternate,
oval.

FLOWERS
male drooping, stalked
heads; female in pairs.

FRUIT
four inside a prickly
brown husk,
September–October.
When ripe this opens
into four lobes, thus
liberating the brown,
three-sided nuts.

HABITAT
widespread and common
throughout the British
Isles, especially on chalky
soils.

Beech dominates the chalk soils of southern England and is associated with a number of species of fungi. The beech is a native species, and has long provided a source of fuel, although it did not gain popularity as a material for construction or furniture until the 18th Century. Since then it has become an extremely popular in kitchens, albeit for building units aι laying floors rather than for its culinary delights.

However, the botanical name Fagus originates from a Greek word meaning 'to eat', but the beech nut or mast is better known as a food for livestock rather then humans. This does not mean to say that the mast is unpalatable – raw, or roasted, and salted, it tastes not unlike young walnut. But the nuts are very small, and the collection and peeling of enough to make an acceptable meal is a tiresome business. This is also an obstacle to the rather more interesting use of beechmast as a source of vegetable oil. Although I have never tried the extraction process myself, mainly because of a lack of suitable equipment, it has been widely used in mainland Europe, particularly in times of economic hardship.

Although beech trees only fruit every three or four years, each tree produces a prodigious quantity of mast, and there is rarely any difficulty in

finding enough. It should be gathered as early as possible, before the squirrels have taken it, and before it has had a chance to dry out. The three-faced nuts should be cleaned of any remaining husks, dirt or leaves and then ground, shells and all, in a small oil mill. (For those with patience, a mincing machine or a strong blender should work as well.) The resulting pulp should be put inside a fine muslin bag and then in a press or under a heavy weight to extract the oil.

For those able to get this far,

the results should be worthwhile. Every 500g (1lb) of nuts yields as much as 85ml (3fl oz) of oil. The oil itself is rich in fats and proteins, and provided it is stored in well-sealed containers, will keep fresh considerably longer than many other vegetable fats.

Beechnut oil can be used for frying, like any other cooking oil. Its most exotic application is probably beechnut butter, which is still made in some rural districts in the United States, and for which there was a patent issued in this country during the reign of George I.

DESCRIPTION
A tall, uneven,
deciduous tree to 30m
(100ft).

LEAVES
single, spear-shaped,
serrated.

FLOWERS
catkins have yellow male
flowers towards the end;
green female part below.

FRUIT
two or three carried in
spherical green cases
with long spines,
October–November.

HABITAT
Well-distributed
throughout England,
though scattered in
Scotland. Fairly common
in woods and parks.

Sweet Chestnut
Castanea sativa

We have the Romans to thank for this delicious nut which when roasted on a fire at home, or smelt cooking in a brazier on the of a corner busy street while Christmas shopping, has became as much a part of the great chilly British autumn as scarves and mittens.

The best chestnut trees are the straight, old ones whose leaves turn brown early. These are not to be confused with the horse chestnut (*Aesculus hippocastanum*), whose inedible conkers look very similar to sweet chestnuts inside their spiny husks. In fact the trees are not related – *Castanea sativa* is more closely related to the oak. The trees will be covered with the prickly fruit as early as September, and small specimens of the nuts to come will be blown down early in the next month. Do not be tempted to collect these, as they are undeveloped and will shrivel in a day or two.

The ripe nuts begin to fall in late October, and can be helped on their way with a few judiciously thrown sticks. Opening the prickly husks can

be a painful business, and for the early part of the crop it is as well to take a pair of gloves and some strong boots, the latter for splitting the husks underfoot, the former for extracting the fruits. The polished brown surface of the ripe nuts uncovered by the split husk is positively alluring. You will want to stamp on every husk you see, and rummage down through the leaves and spines to see if the reward is glinting there.

Don't shy away from eating the nuts raw. If the stringy pith is peeled away as well as the shell then most of the bitterness will go with them. However, roasting transforms them, giving them the sweetness and bulk of a tropical fruit. As is the case with so much else in this book, the excitement lies as much in the rituals of preparation as in the food itself. Chestnut roasting is an institution. To do it efficiently at home, slit the skins, and put the nuts in the hot ash of an open fire or close to the red coals – save one, which is put in uncut, and when this explodes the others are ready. The explosion is fairly ferocious, scattering hot shrapnel over the room, so sit well back from the fire and make sure all the other nuts have been slit.

Chestnuts are a highly versatile vegetable. They can be pickled, candied, or made into an amber with breadcrumbs and egg yolk. Boiled with Brussels sprouts they were Goethe's favourite dish. Chopped, stewed and baked with red cabbage, they make a rich vegetable pudding. Rose Elliot makes a wonderful chestnut and mushroom casserole. Cooked and peeled nuts are stewed with onions, leeks, carrots and celery – and mushrooms of course – together with a generous sprig of fresh thyme. She also has a recipe for chestnuts with Savoy cabbage and sage, another warming autumn dish especially when served with some creamy mashed potato.

Chestnut purée is a versatile way to use the nuts. Shell and peel the chestnuts, and boil them in a thin stock for about 40 minutes. Strain off the liquid and then rub the nuts through a sieve or process them in a liquidiser. The resulting puree can be seasoned and used as substitute for potatoes, or form the basis of stuffings, soups and sweets, such as chestnut fool.

A more elaborate way of storing the nuts is to turn them into flour as is done in some parts of the Mediterranean. You will need to collect a good number of young chestnuts and store them in a warm, dry, well-ventilated room for a couple of months. They must be individually shelled and ground as finely as possible. The flour is fragrant and excellent in cakes and breads, but can be reluctant to rise and is probably best mixed with an equal amount of ordinary wheat flour.

Oak, English Oak
Quercus robur

DESCRIPTION
A deciduous tree, up to 35m (115ft), with a broad, domed crown.

LEAVES
Alternate with irregular lobes.

FLOWERS
appear in late spring; male catkins hang from terminal buds, May.

FRUIT
acorns in clusters.

HABITAT
common throughout deciduous woodland in Britain and Europe.

One of our most common native tree species, oaks have formed part of our folklore and history for centuries. The nuts however, are not as palatable as hazel or chestnuts, and like beechmast, have been more commonly used as animal fodder. Acorns have been used as human food in times of famine.

The raw kernels are forbiddingly bitter to most palates, but chopped and roasted they can be used as a substitute for almonds.

In Europe the most common use of acorns has been in the roast form as a substitute for coffee, and was recommended for this role during the war.

Medlar
Mespilus germanica

DESCRIPTION
deciduous, to 6m (20ft).

LEAVES
alternate, crinkled, white hairs beneath.

FLOWERS
five white petals with longer green sepals, May–June.

FRUIT
resembles a giant brown rosehip, with the five-tailed calyx protruding from the head of the fruit like a crown.

HABITAT
occurs only very occasionally in hedgerows in southern England.

Largely confined to old gardens, and occasionally found in hedgerows, the medlar often grows in gnarled, eccentric shapes produced by the wood's sensitivity to the wind. The curious fact about the medlar is that its fruits

need to be half-rotten – or 'bletted' – before they are edible. This seems to be the result of our climate not being warm enough to ripen the fruits. When the fruits are fully bletted, usually not before the November frosts, the brown flesh can be scraped out of the skin and eaten with cream and sugar. The fruits can also be baked whole, like apples, or made into jelly.

Rowan, Mountain Ash

Sorbus aucuparia

DESCRIPTION
A small tree, up to 20m
(65ft) with fairly smooth
grey bark.

LEAVES
alternate, toothed,
leaflets in 5–10 pairs.

FLOWERS
small, white in umbel.

FRUIT
·large clusters of small
orange berries,
August–November.

HABITAT
widespread and common
in dry woods and rocky
places, especially in the
north and west of the
British Isles.

The rowan is a favourite urban tree, and is planted in great numbers along the edges of residential highways providing a welcome splash of colour. In the wild the rowan likes moist, acid soils and is most common in the north and west of Britain. The trees are easy to identify: their clusters of brilliant orange fruits are unmistakable in almost every setting: against grey limestone in the uplands, or the deep evergreen of Scots pine on wintry heaths. Unless the birds have got there first, rowan berries can hang on the trees until January. They are best picked in October, when they have their full colour but have not yet become mushy.

The best way to pick them is to cut the clusters whole from the trees, trim off any excess stalk, and then make a jelly in the usual way, with the addition of a little chopped crab apple to provide the pectin; crab apples often grow in close proximity to rowan. The jelly is deliciously dark orange, with a sharp marmalade flavour, and is perfect with game and lamb.

Rowan berries have also been brewed into ale and distilled into alcohol, and have been used as bait by trappers to catch birds.

Wild Service tree

Sorbus torminalis

DESCRIPTION
deciduous, up to 25m (80ft), a sign ancient woodland.

LEAVES
alternate, deeply toothed, in pairs.

FLOWERS
white branched clusters, May–June.

FRUIT
brown and speckled, 12–18mm.

HABITAT
largely confined to ancient woods and hedgerows on limestone soils and stiff clays in the Midlands and south.

Widely eaten in Neolithic times, the berries must have been a welcome harvest before other sources of sugar were available. In areas where the tree was relatively widespread (such as the Weald of Kent) they continued to be a popular dessert fruit up to the beginning of this century. The fruits were gathered before they had bletted and strung up in clusters around a stick, which was hung up indoors, often by the hearth. They were picked off and eaten as they ripened, like sweets.

The tree is also known as the Chequer Tree, with links to the traditional pub name 'Chequers'. This can be traced back to Roman times when the chequer board was the symbol for an inn or tavern. In the area around Kent there are many pubs with the name 'Chequers' – 12 in the Canterbury telephone book alone. The berries were also used to make alcoholic drinks, either steeping the berries in a spirit such as gin, or making a type of wine.

I have the house recipe for a wine-type drink served at the Chequers Inn at Smarden:

'Pick off in bunches in October – Hang on strings like onions (looks like swarms of bees) – hang till ripe. Cut off with scissors close to checkers [berries] – put in stone or glass jars – Put sugar on – 1lb to 5lb of checkers – Shake up well. Keep airtight until juice comes to the top. The longer kept the better – Can add brandy. Drink. Then eat berries!'

The bunched red berries of the service tree's relative Whitebeam, *S. aria*, are edible as soon as they begin to blet, although they are rather disappointing. John Evelyn recommended mixing them with new wine and honey. The name whitebeam or 'white tree' is derived from the pale undersides of the leaves, which flash with silver when ruffled by the wind.

BELOW
Whitebeam, *Sorbus aria*.

Sloe, Blackthorn

Prunus spinosa

DESCRIPTION
A stiff, dense shrub up to
6m (20ft) high, with
long thorns.

LEAVES
alternate, oval.

FLOWERS
small and pure white and
appear before the leaves,
March–April.

FRUIT
a small, round, very dark
blue berry covered when
young with a paler
bloom.

HABITAT
widespread and abundant
in woods and hedgerows
throughout the British
Isles, though thinning
out in the north of
Scotland.

*' … These beauty-describing sloes have a little plum-like pulp,
which covers a little roundish stone, pretty nearly as hard as
iron, with a small kernel inside of it. This pulp which I have
eaten many times when I was a boy until my tongue clove to
the roof of my mouth and my lips were pretty near glued
together, is astringent beyond the powers of alum.'*
William Cobbett, 1825

As vividly described by William Cobbett in his wonderful biography of the Blackthorn, the wild sloe is indeed the tartest, most acid berry you will ever taste. Curiously though, we know that a barrowload of sloe-stones were collected during the excavation of a Neolithic lake village at Glastonbury. Were they used for dyeing or eating?

For all its eye-watering acidity, the sloe is a very useful fruit: it makes a clear, sprightly jelly, and that most agreeable ratafia, sloe gin. The best time to pick sloes for this drink is immediately after the first frost, when the skins have softened and 'bletted' and have become more permeable. Sloe gin made at this time will, providentially, just be ready in time for Christmas. Pick about 500g (1lb) of the marble-sized berries (do use a glove

as the spines are stiff and sharp). If they have not been through a first frost, pierce the skin of each with a skewer, to help the gin and the juices mingle more easily. Mix the sloes with half their weight of sugar, and then half fill the bottles with this mixture. Pour gin into the bottles until they are nearly full, and seal tightly. Store for at least two months, and shake occasionally to help dissolve and disperse the sugar. The result is a brilliant, deep pink liqueur, sour-sweet and refreshing.

Wild Cherry
Prunus avium

A beautiful tree in the spring time, and again in autumn when the leaves turn yellow and red, the fruit of the wild cherry can be either sweet or bitter.

These are the best fruits to use for cherry brandy. Put as many as you can find in a bottle with a couple of tablespoons of sugar, and top up with brandy. After 3–4 months you will have a treat waiting in your larder.

DESCRIPTION
A lofty tree, up to 30m (100ft) with shining, reddish-brown bark.

LEAVES
alternate, oval, sharply toothed.

FLOWERS
five white petals; appear in clusters of 2–6 April–May.

FRUIT
resembles a small, dark red, cultivated cherry.

HABITAT
widespread and frequent in hedgerows an woods, especially beech.

Bullace, Damsons and Wild Plums
Prunus spp.

DESCRIPTION
Believed to be a hybrid of Blackthorn (*P. spinosa*) and Cherry Plum (*P. cerasifolia*); gives rise to a number of different fruit trees.

LEAVES
alternate, oval, toothed.

FLOWERS
five white petals; appear in clusters of 2–3, March–May.

HABITAT
woods and hedgerows.

Wild Plum
Prunus domestica agg.

Wild plums can be used instead of their cultivated counterparts in pies and jams and autumn puddings (see p.145), and can also be used to make drinks in the same way as sloes.

Wild plums make excellent dark jams, and the French jam specialist Gisèle Tronche has pointed out how the addition of a little ground cumin seed and aniseed can improve conventional recipes. Alternatively try her late autumn, wild fruit *humeur noir*, which she describes as having 'the colour of a good, healthy, black-tempered funk' (see right).

FAR RIGHT ABOVE
Ripe damsons

RIGHT
Wild plums, *Prunus* spp

FAR RIGHT BELOW
Victoria plums

Bullace

Prunus domestica ssp. *institia*

A wild species with downy, spiny twigs and dark purple fruits. Leaves are hairy on both sides. The damson is a cultivated species derived from the bullace, but this is also naturalised in Britain and the fruits are indistinguishable from the bullace. Indeed, the majority of wild plums found in the countryside are either seeded from garden trees, or are reverted orchard specimens.

Cultivated Plum

Prunus domestica

Characterised by spineless, sparsely hairy twigs, and large, sweet, juicy fruit.

Greengage

Prunus domestica ssp. *italica*

Hairy, spiny twigs, yellow fruit. Leaves hairless above.

Wild fruit jam

Crush together 800g (2lb) of dark damsons and 200g (8oz) of sugar, and leave overnight.

Boil together 200g (8oz) elderberries and 600g (1½lb) blackberries for ten minutes. Add the damsons, another 600g (1½lb) sugar, a tablespoon of cider vinegar and the juice of one lemon, and bring to the boil again. Cook for about an hour until the desired consistency is reached.

Pour into jars, leave to cool and then seal.

Elder

Sambucus nigra

DESCRIPTION
A tall, fast-growing shrub
up to 10m (33ft), with a
corky bark.

LEAVES
usually in groups of five;
large, dark-green and
slightly toothed.

FLOWERS
umbels of numerous tiny
cream-white flowers.

FRUITS
clusters of small, reddish-
black berries,
August–October.

HABITAT
widespread and common
in woods hedgerows and
waste places.

Elder fruits can be used in a number of cooked dishes which eliminates any unpleasant aftertaste. The berries are ripe when the clusters begin to turn upside-down. Gather the clusters whole by cutting them from the stems, picking only those where the very juicy berries have not started to wrinkle or melt. Wash them well, and strip them from the stalks with a fork. They are good added whole to apple pies, or added as a make-weight to blackberry jelly. (Both berries are on the bush at the same time, so if you are making this they can be gathered straight into the same basket.)

My favourite recipe is for Pontack sauce, a relic from those days when every retired military gentleman carried his patent sauce as an indispensable part of his luggage. There are a number of different variants, particularly from the hunting country in the Midlands. This one from Leicestershire probably used claret instead of vinegar in the original.

Pontack sauce

500ml (1 pint) boiling vinegar
(or claret)
500ml (1 pint) elderberries
1 tsp salt
1 blade mace
40 peppercorns
12 cloves
1 onion finely chopped
½ tsp ginger

1 Pour the vinegar (or claret) over the elderberries in a stone jar or casserole dish. Cover and allow to stand overnight in an oven at very low heat.

2 Next day, pour off the liquid, put it in a saucepan with the salt, mace, peppercorns, cloves, onion and ginger. Boil for 10 minutes and then bottle securely with the spices.

The sauce was supposed to be kept for seven years before use. My patience ran out after seven days, but having made rather a large bottle, I can report a distinct improvement in richness after the first few years! It has a fine fruity taste, a little like thick punch, and is especially good with liver.

To see the mangy, decaying skeletons of elders in late autumn and winter, you would not think the bush was any use to man nor beast. Nor would the acrid stench of the young leaves in spring change your opinion. But by the end of June the whole shrub is covered with great sprays of sweet-smelling flowers, for which there are probably more uses than any other single species of blossom. Even in orthodox medicine they have an acknowledged role as an ingredient in skin ointments and eye lotions.

Elder flowers can be munched straight off the branch on a hot summer's day, and taste as frothy as a glass of ice-cream soda. Something even closer to that drink can be made by putting a bunch of elder flowers in a jug with boiling water, straining off the liquid when cool, and sweetening.

Cut the elder flower clusters whole, with about 2 in (5cm) of stem attached to them (the stems are needed for one recipe, see right). Always check they are free from insects, and discard any that are badly infested. The odd grub or two can be removed by hand. But never wash the flowers as this will remove much of the fragrance. The young buds can be pickled or added to salads. The flowers themselves, separated from the stalks, make what is indisputably the best sparkling wine besides champagne.

Jellies and jams form because of a chemical reaction between a substance called pectin, present in the fruit, and sugar. The pectin (and the acid in the fruit which also plays a part in the process), tends to be most concentrated when the fruit is under-ripe, but at this stage the flavour is not fully developed, so the best time to pick the fruit is when it is just ripe. Elder flowers make a wonderful preserve with gooseberries. Gooseberries are rich in pectin and acid and set easily. Some fruits such as strawberries and blackberries contain less pectin and require additional pectin before they will set. This can be provided by using lemon juice or some crab apples.

To make the preserve, trim off as much of the bitter stalk as you can, and have ready four flower heads for each pound of gooseberries. Top, tail and wash the gooseberries in the usual way, and put them into a pan with 500ml (1 pint) of water for every 500g (1lb) of fruit. Simmer for half and hour, mashing the fruit to a pulp as you do so. Add one pound of sugar for each pound of fruit, stir rapidly until dissolved, and bring to the boil. Then add the elder flowers tied in muslin, and boil rapidly until the settling point is reached. Remove the flowers and pot in the usual way. The flavour is quite transformed from that of plain gooseberry jam, and reminiscent of muscat grapes. It is good with ice-cream and other sweets.

Elder flower fritters

4 tbsp flour

I egg

I ½ cupfuls water

Elderflower heads (retain short

stalks for dipping)

Oil for frying

Mint

Sugar for dusting

1 Make up the batter with the flour, egg and water

2 Hold the flower head by the stalk and dip into the batter. Shake off any excess and then deep-fry until golden-brown

3 Trim off the excess stalk and serve with sugar and mint.

DESCRIPTION
A sprawling evergreen
shrub, up to 1.5m (5ft)
high.

LEAVES
holly-like with sharp
spines.

FLOWERS
fragrant, yellow, uneven
petals.

FRUIT
dark, white-bloomed, in
bunches like miniature
grapes.

HABITAT
often naturalised in a
number of places in open
woodland and game
coverts.

Oregon Grape
Mahonia aquifolium

A member of the barberry family, originally from western North America, oregon grapes are planted to provide cover and food for pheasants. The fruit can be eaten raw, and has been eaten as food in the United States, though they are rather acid. They are best made into a jelly.

DESCRIPTION
Tall, greyish-green
annual, up to 1m (3ft)
high.

LEAVES
stalked, lower leaves
lobed and bristly.

FLOWERS
yellow, June–August.

FRUIT
seed pods pressed against
the stem.

HABITAT
quite common as an
escape from cultivation
on waysides and waste
places.

Black Mustard
Brassica nigra

Black mustard seeds have long been used to provide a tang for our cooking. Collecting the seeds can be a painstaking process, but a pinch will liven up Welsh rarebit, and 25g (1oz) will make a lemon and mustard seed chutney. Thinly slice four onions and five lemons, sprinkle with salt and leave for 12 hours. Add the mustard seeds, a teaspoon of allspice, 500g (1lb) sugar, 100g (4oz) raisins and 500ml (1 pt) cider vinegar. Bring to the boil and simmer for an hour. Transfer to jars and seal when cool.

DESCRIPTION
Hairy annual, 30–60cm
(1–2 ft).

FLOWER
deep scarlet often with a
dark centre, petals floppy,
June–October.

FRUIT
seed pods are hairless and
flat-topped like an
inverted cone.

HABITAT
widespread and abundant
in arable fields and by
roadsides. Becomes
scarcer in Wales, north-
west England and
northern Scotland.

Corn Poppy, Field Poppy

Papaver rhoeas

Poppies and cornfields have long been associated in our consciousness, from the Roman corn goddess Ceres, who was depicted with a bunch of poppies in one hand, to Monet's atmospheric, sun-drenched landscapes. The plant probably arrived in Britain with our first Neolithic settlers, and thrived in the countryside. Aggressive use of herbicides to ensure a plentiful supply of food following the Second World War virtually eliminated the poppy from our fields, and the plant became confined to roadsides and waste places. Now, however, changes in farming practices, and a revival of interest in the flower, has heralded its return to our landscape.

Superstitions about the supposed poisonous nature of the flower still persist, notably the belief that the seed heads contain opium. In fact no part of the common field poppy are narcotic, least of all the dry seeds. It is the Asian species *Papaverum somniferum* from which opium is derived. Yet the dry ripe seeds of the opium poppy are entirely edible, and indeed are the poppy seeds of commerce, used extensively in baking. Corn poppy seeds make an acceptable, though less flavorsome, substitute.

The seeds heads start to dry in September, and are ready for picking

when they are grey-brown in colour, and have a number of small holes just below the edge of the flat top. The seed in ripe heads can be readily shaken out of these holes.

Pick a handful of these heads, and put them straight into a paper bag. Remove the seeds by inverting the heads and shaking them into the bag. Any that cling to their contents are not really ripe. Poppy seeds are extensively used in European and Middle Eastern cookery.

DESCRIPTION
thorny plant with
arching stems to 3m
(10ft).

LEAVES
pairs of toothed leaflets.

FLOWERS
pink or white, June–July.

FRUIT
orange-red, oblong, up to
2.5cm (1in), late
August–November.

HABITAT
hedgerows, rough grass,
scrub.

Rose-hip

Rosa canina

The austerity of the Second World War forced the British government to exploit one of our native wild fruits, which went on to become one of the great success stories of wild food use. It is the only completely wild fruit which supports a national commercial enterprise – the production of rose-hip syrup.

The lack of citrus fruit and the threat of the seaman's enemy, scurvy, or Vitamin C deficiency, meant that for the first time the potentialities of rose-hips as a source of Vitamin C were taken seriously on a national scale. However, rose-hips had been used as a food for centuries before that. When cultivated fruit was scarce in the Middle Ages, rose-hips were used as a dessert. A recipe from 1730 explains how this hard, unlikely berry was transformed into a filling for tarts. The hips were first split in half, and the pith and seeds thoroughly cleaned out. Then the skins were put to stand in an earthenware pot until they were soft enough to rub through a sieve. (Notice that this was done without the use of heat or liquid.) The resulting purée was mixed with its own weight of sugar, warmed until the sugar melted, and then potted.

In 1941 the Ministry of Health put forward a scheme for collection of rose-hips which had been found to contain 20 times the amount of Vitamin C in oranges, and in that year 120,000 kg (120 tons) were gathered by voluntary collectors. The next year the scheme was transferred to the Vegetable Drugs Committee of the Ministry of Supply and 349,500 kg (344 tons) were gathered. By 1943 the redoubtable County Herb Committees were brought in to organise the collection, and for the next three years the harvest averaged 457,000 kg (350 tons). The resulting syrup was sold through ordinary retailers at a controlled price of 1s 9d (9 new pence) for a 150g (6oz) bottle. Mothers and children were able to obtain it in larger quantities, and at reduced prices, from Welfare Clinics.

The syrup is really the beginning of all useful rose-hip recipes, and making it is the simplest way of filtering out the prickly seed, which can be a dangerous internal irritant. These are the meticulous directions given by the Ministry of Food during the War for 2 lb (1kg) of hips:

Have ready 3 pints [1.5l] boiling water, mince the hips in a coarse mincer, drop immediately into the boiling water or if possible mince the hips directly into the boiling water and again bring to the boil. Stop heating and put aside for 15 minutes. Pour into a flannel or linen crash jelly bag and allow to drip until the bulk of the liquid has come through. return the residue to the saucepan, add 1½ pints [750ml] of boiling water, stir and allow to stand for 10 minutes. Pour back into the jelly bag and allow to drip. To make sure all the sharp hairs are removed, put back the first half cupful of liquid and allow to drip through again. Put the mixed juice into a clean saucepan and boil down until the juice measures about 1½ pints [750ml], then add 1¾ lb [900g] of sugar and boil for a further 5 minutes. Pour into hot, sterile bottles and seal at once. If corks are used these should have been boiled for ¼ hour just previously and after insertion coated with melted paraffin wax. It is advisable to use small bottles as the syrup will not keep for more than a week or two once the bottle is opened. Store in a dark cupboard.
Hedgerow Harvest, Ministry of Food, 1943

ABOVE
Rose-hips in hoar frost.

The resulting syrup can be used a natural alternative to fruit squashes, or as a flavouring for natural yoghurt or ice-cream.

DESCRIPTION
A prickly shrub, usually growing in straggly, tangled clumps.

LEAVES
prickly and toothed, and turn reddish-purple in the autumn.

FLOWERS
5 white or pinkish petals.

FRUIT
comprises a number of drupelets, turning from green to red to a deep purple-black, August–October.

HABITAT
widespread and abundant in woods, hedges, waste places and heaths.

Blackberry

Rubus fruticosus

We have eaten blackberries since Neolithic times: seeds have been found in the stomach of man dug up from the Essex clay. Blackberrying carries with it a little of the urban dweller's myth of country life: abundance, harvest, a sense of season, and just enough discomfort to quicken the senses. Maybe it is the scuffing and the scratches that are the real attraction: the proof of satisfying toil against unruly nature.

Everyone has their favourite picking habits and recipes, and these are better guides than anything a book can say. So I will confine myself to a few of the lesser known facts about the fruit.

Blackberry bushes spread in a curious way. Each cane begins by growing erectly, but then curves downwards until its tip touches the ground. Here the shoot takes root, and a clump of new canes soon forms. The berries themselves grow in large clusters at the end of the older shoots, which die after two or three years' cropping. The lowest berry – right at the tip of the stalk – is the first to ripen and is the sweetest and fattest of all. Eat it raw. A few weeks later, the other berries near the end ripen; these are less juicy, but are still good for jam and pies. The small berries further up the stalk often do not ripen until October. They are hard and slightly bitter and are only really useful if cooked with other fruit.

Even more variety is found from bush to bush. There are reckoned to be at least 400 microspecies in Britain, all differing slightly in flavour, sweetness, fruiting time, nutritional content and size. Blackberries can occur with the savours of grape, plum and even apple. Some varieties have more dietary fibre, weight for weight, than wholemeal bread. If any wild variety does take your fancy, try growing a cutting in the garden. It should bear fruit after a couple of years.

There are any number of recipes which make use of blackberries: pies, fruit fools and salads, jellies (they need a little extra pectin), and jams. A good way of serving them fresh is to leave them to steep overnight in red wine.

The most delicious blackberry product I know is a junket made from nothing other than blackberry juice. Remove the juice from the very ripest berries with the help of a juice extractor, or by pressing them through several layers of muslin. Then simply allow the thick, dark juice to stand undisturbed in a warm room. Do not stir or cool the juice, or add anything to it. In a few hours it will have set to the consistency of a light junket, and can be eaten with cream and sweet biscuits.

Autumn pudding

8–10 slices of brown wholemeal bread
Milk
600g (1½ lb) autumn fruits, such as
blackberries, stoned sloes, bullaces,
elderberries and crab apples
100g (4oz) caster sugar or dark honey

1 Cut 8–10 fairly thin slices of bread and remove the crusts. Moisten with milk and line the sides and bottom of a deep pudding basin (make sure the slices overlap well, so that they will hold together when turned out).

2 Fill the basin with a mixture of dark fruits, especially blackberries, together with a few stoned sloes and bullaces, elderberries, and chopped crab apples. These should have been cooked for about ten minutes and sweetened with dark honey or caster sugar to taste.

3 Cover the top with more slices of moistened bread, and then with greaseproof paper. Put a weight on top of the paper and leave the pudding to stand in the refrigerator overnight.

4 Turn out and serve with crème fraiche, ice-cream or custard.

Dewberry
Rubus caesius

DESCRIPTION
Hairy, sprawling
perennial, growing up to
40cm (12in) with weak
prickles.

FLOWERS
white, May–September.

HABITAT
widespread and frequent
in bushy and grassy
places, especially in
eastern England.

The dewberry is distinguished from the blackberry by its smaller fruits, fewer segments and the fine bloom that covers them. They are also so juicy that they can be difficult to pick without bursting, but persevere as they are worth it, dipped in sugar and cream.

Cloudberry
Rubus chamaemorus

DESCRIPTION
A low, creeping shrub to
20cm (8in).

LEAVES
rounded, lobed.

FLOWERS
five white petals, solitary,
June–August.

FRUIT
round, red at first, orange
when ripe.

HABITAT
found in peatland soils,
chiefly in mountainous
areas of the north.

The cloudberry has always been a shy fruiter in this country (unlike in Scandinavia, for instance). It is a subalpine species, confined to bogs and moors in the north of England and Wales, and Scotland.

In the Berwyn mountains in Wales, an unusual tradition commemorated this scarcity, and persisted up until the end of the 19th Century. Inhabitants of Llanrhaiadr believed that a quart of cloudberries was the wage that St Dogfan was due for his spiritual ministry, and anyone who could bring such a quantity to the parson on St Dogfan's Day had his tithes (taxes) remitted for the year.

The berries are red at first, ripening to a delicate marmalade-orange. They have been used in the northern areas of Britain for puddings and jams, and can be included in any dish that is conventionally made from blackberries or raspberries, but they make for fairly indifferent eating. In Sweden, the berries are eaten fresh, mashed with sugar.

Rock Samphire
Crithmum maritimum

DESCRIPTION
A squat, bushy plant growing up to 30cm (1ft) high; stems hairless and solid.

LEAVES
fleshy grey-green, in narrow, untoothed leaflets.

FLOWERS
yellow umbels, July–October.

HABITAT
frequent on rocky coasts in the south and west.

A plant of rocky coasts; you might catch the warm but slightly sulphurous smell of rock samphire before you see it. Both stems and leaves can be used: either boiled like a vegetable for about ten minutes, and served with melted butter. To eat, suck the fleshy parts away from the stringy veins (remember to remove any leaves that have begun to turn slimy, and any hard parts of the stalk before cooking). Or as a pickle, soaked in salt water for 2–3 hours, drained and then cooked in wine vinegar, water and salt. Once cooled it is stored in jars with fresh vinegar, water and salt so it remains green.

BELOW
Rock samphire at Kimmeridge, Dorset.

Samphire hash

100g (4oz) samphire chopped
1 handful diced pickled cucumber and capers
500ml (1 pint) stock
2 tbsp wine vinegar
1 lemon
Slivers of butter
1 egg yolk
Pepper and nutmeg to taste

1 Mix the chopped samphire with the pickled cucumbers and capers

2 Mix the stock with the wine vinegar, the juice and peel of the lemon, and the pepper and nutmeg, bring to the boil and then add the samphire. Simmer for half an hour.

3 Take off the boil and gradually add slivers of butter and the yolk of an egg, stirring constantly until the mixture thickens.

Fennel

Foeniculum vulgare

DESCRIPTION
Tall, greyish perennial to
2m (6½ft); strong-
smelling, solid stems.

LEAVES
threadlike and aromatic.

FLOWERS
clusters of mustard-
yellow blossoms,
July–October.

HABITAT
local in the south of
England, Midlands, East
Anglia and Wales. Less
common in Scotland. On
cliffs, waste ground and
damp places, especially
near the sea.

More than likely we have the Romans to thank for the exotic plumes of fennel we see on our waysides, as they prized it for its medicinal and culinary properties, and probably introduced it to this country. It is now widely naturalised, especially on damp coastal roadsides. Its umbels of yellow flowers and smooth, threadlike leaves are elegantly soft, giving the plant a curiously foppish air beside the hairy yokels it shares its living space with. Crush the leaves in your hand and they give off a powerful aromatic odour, reminiscent of aniseed. On a hot summer's day this is enough to betray the plant's presence, for the cool tang stands out from the heavy, sweet musk of hogweed and elder like a throwback to a sharp April morning.

Fennel occurs throughout the southern half of the British Isles, on cliffs as much as in dank meadows, but it tends to grow in rather localised patches. All parts of the plant are edible, from the stalks – if your teeth are strong enough – to the rather sparse bulb. (The larger fennel bulbs available in the shops belong to cultivated Florence fennel *Foeniculum vulgare* var. *dulce*.) They all have a fresh, nutty flavour. But it is the thinner stalks, leaf sprays and seeds that are the most useful.

The green parts of the plant should be cut with a sharp knife as early in the summer as possible, and some (stalks included) hung up to dry for the winter. Fennel smells stronger as it dries, and after a few weeks a good-sized bunch will be powerful enough to scent a whole room. The seeds should be gathered late in October, just before they are fully dry. The leaves are popular in cooking, particularly with fish, though the tradition of using it in this way could derive from nothing more than the plant's preference for

BELOW
Fennel, Barnham Overy,
Staithe, Norfolk.

Okrochka

250 ml (10 fl oz) yoghurt (natural or apple)
250 ml (10 fl oz) milk
1 cup diced fresh cucumber
½ cup chopped pickled cucumber or gerkin
½ cup diced cooked chicken
One handful of finely-chopped fennel leaves
Fresh summer herbs (mint, parsley, chives)
Two hard-boiled eggs, chopped
Salt and pepper to taste

1 Mix the yoghurt and the milk in a good sized bowl.

2 Add the cucumber, pickled cucumber (or gerkin), chicken and fennel, together with a little fresh, mint, parsley and chives.

3 Season with salt and pepper and put in the fridge for at least two hours.

4 Before serving, add two roughly-chopped hard-boiled eggs to the soup and sprinkle the surface with a little more black pepper and fresh herbs.

This exotic cold soup from Greece can really charm and make use of the cool flavour of fennel. It is a perfect dish on a warm summer evening, and utilises some other wild summer herbs you may gather.

coastal areas. Chopped fennel and gooseberries make a classic sauce to accompany mackerel.

Fennel was one of the Anglo-Saxon herbalists' nine sacred herbs, and in *The Englishman's Doctor* published in 1608 the seeds were valued for the following reason:

'In Fennel-seed, this vertue you shall find,
Foorth of your lower parts to drive the winde'.

The digestive properties of the seeds are still recognised, and are sometimes served at the end of Indian meals.

The finely-chopped green leaves are also good to add to liver, potato salad and parsnips.

Fungi

Wild and exotic fungi are becoming increasingly prized and more commonly found on restaurant menus, supermarket shelves and in our kitchens. However, their strange shapes and unusual textures often command a premium in terms of price – what better than to venture out into the woods and find your own. There are over 100 edible species growing in this country, and although they do vary in terms of quality of taste and texture, all contain a source of protein and Vitamin D. Different species of fungi fruit at different times of the year – there is generally at least one good edible fungi available in each season. Where they are found is determined by the way in which fungi grow. They are characterised by the fact that they do not contain chlorophyll, and as a result are unable to produce their own carbohydrates. Therefore they must live off those produced by other plants. Soil rich in root structures or decaying plant litter is a good environment for fungi, as are mature woodland and well-established pasture. Fungi also thrive in warm, damp conditions, and so a year that begins with a long, fine summer, and continues with a wet, mild autumn, is likely to produce a bumper harvest. In wet summers look for fungi in woodland clearings; in dry summers try your luck in shady, damper areas.

ABOVE
Old beech stump covered with fungi, Bramshaw Wood, New Forest.

RIGHT
Bay bolete, Xerocomus badius

Picking rules

To make the most of wild fungi, follow a few simple guidelines on picking, preparation and storing.

1. Only pick fungi which satisfy all criteria on size, colour, time of year and environment given in this book. There are a number of other guides available which can help you make an accurate identification. Just remember, if you are in any doubt, do not eat it!

2. Do not pick old or decaying specimens or specimens that are too young to be identified accurately.

3. Avoid gathering on very wet days as many fungi absorb water. Moisture will spoil the taste, impair the texture and will accelerate decay.

4. When picking fungi do not cut them or pull them out of the ground. To make a proper identification you need all parts of the fungus to be intact, including the stem (stipe), and any sheath (volva) that surrounds it. The root system of the fungus remains under the ground; what we pick are just the fruits of the fungus, the only part visible above the ground. The best way to pick a fungus without damaging the rest of the plant, is to twist the stipe gently until it breaks free.

5. Cut the earthy part of the stipe away before putting it into your basket to keep all specimens as clean as possible, and make sure the basket is well-ventilated to minimise decay while in transit.

6. Go through all your specimens again before cooking to make sure you have identified them correctly. Again, discard any that you are unsure of. Also check for maggots by cutting the caps in half. It is a good idea also to discard any with white gills as this is a feature of most poisonous *Amanita* species. Also cut away any wet or decaying parts. Clean the fungi by brushing or cutting away dirt, do not wash or peel them.

7. Try just a small portion when sampling anything for the first time, as it may not agree with you.

8. Fungi can be kept in the refrigerator for a few days provided they are young, dry and free from insects. A few species freeze well, such as *Agaricus* and *Boletus* spp. Do not thaw before cooking; fry or boil them in salted water for a few minutes before cooking as for fresh mushrooms. Do not keep them frozen for more than a year. The best way to keep fungi is by drying them; species with a firm texture are best. Small caps can be dried whole, larger ones should be cut into slices up to 2cm (1in) thick. Thread the caps or pieces onto string or wire and keep in a warm dry place, such as an airing cupboard or above a radiator. When dry, store in an airtight container. When you want to reuse them, just soak in water, the fungi will hydrate, and you can use the liquor for cooking.

DESCRIPTION
Resembles a large, round
natural sponge, or the
heart of a cauliflower,
10–20cm (4–8in); colour
varies with age. Pleasant
smell.

FRUITBODY
15–40cm (6–15in)
across, with flat, twisted
and very divided
branches.

HABITAT
at the base of pine
stumps or living trees,
August–November.

Cauliflower Fungus, Brain Fungus

Sparassis crispa

If you are lucky enough to find a *Sparassis* (the Swiss call it 'the Broody hen') it should be cut off from its thick fleshy stalk with a knife. Only young specimens should be gathered as the old ones are tough and bitter.

Cut the *Sparassis* into sections, making it easier to clean, and remove any brown or spongy parts. Wash thoroughly to remove any pine-needles and insects from the folds. One recipe for very young specimens is to bake or fry in a casserole with butter, parsley, a little garlic and some stock and seasoning. They have a delicious mild and pleasantly nutty flavour; it is this flavour that makes a good addition to soups and stews. They can also be deep-fried in batter. They dry well, and older specimens can be dried until brittle, for future use as a flavouring.

The only slightly dangerous species with which *Sparassis* could be confused is *Ramaria formosa* which usually grows with beech. It is rare and has pink rounded branches with yellow tips.

DESCRIPTION
A large, red bracket
fungus 20–40cm
(8–16in) in diameter.

FRUITBODY
tongue-shaped, rough
and sticky becoming
dryer and smoother with
age. Yellow pores exude a
blood-like juice when
bruised.

HABITAT
on old oak or sweet
chestnut,
August–October.

Beefsteak Fungus

Fistulina hepatica

When cut, this bracket fungus looks and feels exactly like raw prime beef; the French name for it means ox-tongue. It occurs occasionally on living trees, especially oak. The top is reddish brown, and the underside is covered with minute yellow pores.

Sadly, the beefsteak fungus does not really fulfil its visual promise, and the meat is rather tough and bitter. It is best chopped small and fried well with some other fairly strongly-flavoured ingredients, such as onions and herbs. Stewing repeatedly in water, with the water being changed each time, can remove the acid that makes the fungus bitter.

DESCRIPTION
Funnel-shaped, 4–10cm
(1½–4in) high, browny-
black in colour.

CAP
hollow to the base, with
a heavy crinkled margin
2–8cm (1–3in); lower
surface of cap continuous
with stem, and smooth or
slightly wrinkled.

GILLS
none.

RING
none.

HABITAT
fairly common in leafy
woods, especially beech
August–November.

Horn of Plenty
Craterellus cornucopoides

The flesh of this species is thin and leathery and tastes of earth when eaten raw, but is highly prized for culinary purposes. When you get it home, check that the base is free from dirt and insects before sautéeing until softened. The caps can then be stuffed, or used in sauces or soups. Horn of plenty is also good for drying.

DESCRIPTION
Medium-sized, 3–8cm
(1–3in), with a short,
stout, whitish stem.

CAP
irregularly shaped, up to
15cm (6in) across,
covered with matt buffish
to pink skin, smooth and
often cracked, like fine
leather, wavy margin.

GILLS
unmistakable tiny teeth,
paler than the cap,
brittle and unequal in
length.

RING
none.

HABITAT
common in all kinds of
woodland,
August–November.

Hedgehog Fungus
Hydnum repandum

The genus *Hydnum* is unique amongst fungi in having spines instead of gills, and all the more common species with this characteristic are edible. Once you have picked the caps, any dirt trapped in the spines can be removed with a knife. It is best to remove the spines completely from older caps.

The hedgehog fungus is the most common *Hydnum* species, and is good to eat once its slightly bitter taste has been removed. This is best done by blanching the chopped fungus for a few minutes and then draining off and discarding the water. Sliced and lightly fried the fungus is good served on toast with a dash of sherry sprinkled over the top. Its firm texture makes it good for freezing (once cooked), and it can also be pickled or fried.

A close relative of the wood hedgehog is *Sarcodon imbricatum*. It is greyish-brown in colour, with a scaly cap with the spiny gill structure of the *Hydnum* family. It occurs occasionally in sandy conifer woods.

FAR RIGHT
Sarcodon imbricatum.

DESCRIPTION
Medium sized, 4–10cm
(1½–4in) high; stem
stout, tinged with blue
and occasionally swollen
at the base.

CAP
flattish with an incurving
marginal edge, 5–12 cm
(2–5in) across, dry to
touch but slightly jellyish
and translucent, pale
brown to greyish in
colour. Flesh white and
firm.

GILLS
crowded, white to
greyish-pink.

RING
none.

HABITAT
not uncommon in grassy
pastures,
October–December.

Field Blewitt, Blue Leg
Lepista saeva

Named after the bluish-violet tinge in their stems, blewitts were one of the few fungi once sold commercially in Britain. The trade was especially strong in the Midlands, and it is from there that the traditional way of cooking blewitts as tripe comes.

Blewitts often grow in pastures in large rings, and it is easy to overlook them in the late autumn, as their flat, irregular caps look like dead leaves scattered over the field. Pick them on a dry day (they are very porous), clean and chop off their stems.

One way to serve this excellent fungus is to cut up the stems finely with an equal amount of onions and pack around the caps with a little chopped sage and bacon fat. Just cover the blewitts with milk and simmer for half an hour. Pour off the liquid, thicken with flour, butter and seasoning, and pour back over the fungi mixture. Simmer for another quarter of an hour, and then serve the whole mixture inside a ring of mashed potatoes, with toast and apple sauce. This way of cooking fungi is probably not entirely fortuitous, for their aromatic taste and jellyish texture are indeed reminiscent of tripe. Fried with onions, and perhaps with some chopped, cooked potato, they also make an

excellent omelette filling. They can also be dried, pickled or frozen.

The woodland equivalent of the field blewitt, the wood blewitt, *Lepista nuda* (see left) is much like the field blewitt but is bluish or violet all over when young, becoming whiter with age. The cap, 5–10cm (2–4in) across turns reddish with age. Do not eat raw as it can be indigestible, but it makes a good stewing fungus.

Honey Fungus
Armillariella mellea

DESCRIPTION
Tufts of honey-brown caps 5–12cm (2–5in), with yellowish stems growing from black 'bootlaces'.

CAP
colour variable, yellow to olive-brown, 2–15cm (1–6in); convex with hairy brownish scales when young, flattening with age.

GILLS
creamy-white, darken with age.

RING
shaggy, yellow.

HABITAT
abundant throughout Britain on tree stumps, roots and buried branches, September–December

A destructive parasite on all kinds of timber, recognisable from the black rhizomes encircling its host, which resemble a network of leather bootlaces.

Collect the caps when young, when the gills are white, and do not eat raw. Blanch before cooking, and then fry slowly. They have a strong flavour and firm texture, and are best served in small quantities on the first tasting as they can be quite rich for some people. Probably best added to stews.

Anise Cap, Aniseed Toadstool
Clitocybe odora

DESCRIPTION
Greenish-blue, medium-small, 4–8cm (1½–3in), stem slender. Strong smell of aniseed.

CAP
3–6cm (1–2in) convex, inrolled, greenish-blue when young; becoming lighter, flatter and wavy with age.

GILLS
cream ageing to grey-green.

HABITAT
with beech and oak, on chalky soils, August–November.

A small fungus which occurs in the litter of mixed woodlands in late summer and autumn. The whole fungus is blue-green in colour, and has a strong, unmistakable smell of aniseed. The aniseed smell persists on drying, and either fresh or dried, the anise cap can used as a flavouring. It is good for flavouring fish in place of fennel.

Parasol Mushroom
Lepiota procera

DESCRIPTION
A large fungus 15–30cm (6–12in) high; stem tall, slender, hollow and bulbous at the base.

CAP
dry, scaly, brown to grey-brown, 10–25cm (4–10in). Domed when young; becomes flatter with age. Always retains dark central prominence.

GILLS
white and detached from the stem.

RING
large, white, double; it eventually becomes completely free of the stem so it can be moved up and down.

HABITAT
occasional in wood margins, grassy clearings, roadsides, July–November.

BELOW RIGHT
Shaggy parasol, *Macrolepiota rhacodes*.

With its large, dry cap the parasol is one of our best edible fungi, and is highly prized by all who go out mushrooming. It is also very distinctive, and can often be seen from afar because of its size and preference for open spaces. The parasol rises closed, held to the stem by its large white ring. It then breaks free and opens like an umbrella. For the best combination of size and tenderness it should be picked when the cap begins to open.

To cook, remove the woody stems, and fry the caps quickly in oil or butter, like field mushrooms. Alternatively, to avoid the caps soaking up too much fat, coat them first in batter or breadcrumbs. The shape of the more mature caps makes them suitable for making into fritters. Prepare the caps by removing the stalks, and wiping clean. Then dip them, whole, into flour, then batter, and deep-fry in oil for about five minutes.

Because of their shape young parasols are also ideal for stuffing: choose specimens that are still cup-shaped, cut off and discard the stems and fill with a sage and onion stuffing (or with mince or sausage meat for a more substantial dish). Arrange them in their natural way up in a baking tray. A small strip of bacon fat can be attached to the top of each parasol with a skewer to add even more flavour. Cook in the oven for about half an hour, basting once or twice.

A lookalike species, the shaggy parasol, *Macrolepiota rhacodes*, is not uncommon on rich ground, through it prefers more shade than the common parasol. It is very similar to the parasol mushroom, but the cap is scalier and the stem quite smooth. The flesh is white but reddens on cutting; it smells stronger than *procera* and slightly sweet. Cook in the same way as for parasol mushroom. Please note this species has been known to cause digestive upsets and rashes on skin.

Shaggy Ink Cap
Coprinus comatus

DESCRIPTION
A tall, shaggy, scaly
fungus, 8–25cm
(3–10in), with a smooth,
white stem.

CAP
white, almost cylindrical
at first, covered with
shaggy woolly scales;
opens to resemble a limp
umbrella, which becomes
smaller with age.

GILLS
white at first, then
darkening from pink to
black as the cap opens,
finally dissolving into an
inky fluid.

RING
small, white, moveable.

HABITAT
common in fields, road
verges, playing fields,
rubbish tips,
June–November.

The shaggy ink cap has a preference for grassland that is managed by humans rather than animals, even in urban areas. It can often be found in large numbers in the short, mown grass by roadsides, and even in the thin stripes between dual carriageways. It comes up like a white busby and can scarcely be mistaken for any other species, save perhaps its close relative *Coprinus atramentarius*. This too is edible but can produce nausea if eaten together with alcohol. *C. atramentarius* can be distinguished by its dirty grey colour, its absence of scales, its generally more slender build and lack of ring.

The shaggy ink cap should be gathered whilst the cap is still closed and the gills pale, and should be cooked as soon as possible after picking, before the cap starts to dissolve. Remove dirt by wiping with a damp cloth.

Once the stems have been removed, they can be fried quickly in oil or butter, or deep-fried in breadcrumbs. Or you can bake them in a very slow casserole with cream or a mustard-flavoured roux for up to an hour. The taste is pleasant and mild, a little like shellfish in texture, but the taste is perhaps too innocuous for some palates.

You can capitalise on their deliquescent nature and turn them into ketchup. Put the young caps into an earthenware pot, pack them down well and sprinkle each layer with salt. When the pot is full, put it in the oven, and simmer for an hour or two, being careful not to lose too much liquid through evaporation. Then strain through muslin, and for each quart of liquid add an ounce of black pepper and a scrape of nutmeg. Boil up again and strain into clean (preferably sterilised) bottles and seal well. The ketchup will keep indefinitely, but should be used quickly once opened.

Field Mushroom
Agaricus campestris

DESCRIPTION
A familiar smell, white mushroom; smells and tastes stronger than cultivated mushrooms. Stem short, white.

CAP
white, dry, firm and domed when young; when mature may become flatter with pale brown scales, 3–10cm (1–4in).

GILLS
initially enclosed in a white veil; first pink, darkening to brown and then black.

RING
thin, transient. In young specimens the ring is joined to the cap.

HABITAT
locally common in pastures and meadows, July–November.

The right combination of temperature, humidity and soil condition can produce a bumper harvest of our most familiar fungus, *Agaricus campestris* and its relatives, and they can appear almost overnight. But, paradoxically, they can be one of the less easy fungi to identify precisely. There is virtually nothing which can be mistaken for a *Sparassis* or a chanterelle, but there are one or two white-capped meadow fungi which can be taken for edible mushrooms by the careless; if you study cultivated mushrooms carefully, and only go for similar pink-gilled sheathless specimens from the wild, you are unlikely to make a mistake.

When you have your mushrooms check them again to make sure there are none with greenish-tinged or warty caps, or with remnants of sheath at the bottom of the stems. And until you are expert at recognising the 'jizz' of mushrooms it is as well to be doubly cautious and cut each specimen in half vertically. Discard any with pure white gills, or that quickly stain pink or yellow. Both common species, the blusher (*Amantia rubescens*), and the yellow-staining mushroom (*Agaricus xanthodermus*, see photograph bottom left), can be mistaken for the field mushroom, and though neither of them is dangerously poisonous, they can cause digestive upsets.

There is no need to peel mushrooms – indeed the taste will be diminished if you do. Simply wipe the caps with a dampish cloth and cut off the base of the stem. The very best way of cooking mushrooms is to fry them in bacon fat as soon as possible after collecting. The secret is to give them no more than three or four minutes in the pan. Field mushrooms tend to contain more water than cultivated, and if they are cooked for too long, they stew in their own liquid and become limp and mushy. Making soup from your wild mushrooms avoids this danger. Simply simmer the chopped caps and stems in a seasoned milk for half an hour with no other ingredients at all. Liquidise in a blender if desired. The result is a smooth, light soup which is good hot or cold. Young field mushrooms can be used raw in salads, and ripe, dark-gilled ones for ketchup. Many other recipes came to light during the mushroom glut of autumn 1976 following the severe drought the same summer.

Mushroom pâté

200g (8oz) field mushrooms

I onion

I tomato

I rasher of bacon (optional)

I egg beaten

I   Chop the mushrooms with the onion, tomato and bacon if using. Cook slowly in a little oil until the mushrooms begin to sweat, and cook for 10 minutes. If the mushrooms give off a great deal of liquid drain some away.

2   Cool, transfer to a blender and blitz until smooth.

3   Return to the pan, add seasoning and herbs to taste, and perhaps a pinch of chilli powder, and the beaten egg. Stir over a low heat until the texture thickens.

4   Refrigerate for at least 12 hours.

The following relatives of the field mushroom can all be treated in similar ways and are all edible and good.

Bleeding Brown Mushroom, *Agaricus haemorrhoidarius.* Common under broad-leaved trees, especially oak, among soil and dead leaves. The cap is hazel-brown with faint scales, 10–12cm (4–6in), gills pink. White flesh turns blood-red on cutting. Double ring. September

Brown Wood Mushroom, *Agaricus sylvaticus.* Common under conifers. Cap is covered with russet-brown scales 5–9cm (2–3½in), gills reddish. White flesh stains orange-red, and then blood-red when cut. Large ring. August–October

Wood Mushroom, *Agaricus sylvicola.* Occasional in deciduous and coniferous woodland. White cap turns yellow and eventually orange, 5–10cm (2–4in), gills pinkish-grey. Flesh white, becoming yellow, aniseed smell. August–November

Agaricus macrosporus. The mushroom of Highland pastures (see photograph above left). Cap fleshy and silky white, 20–30cm (8–12in), remains convex. Flesh thick, white, flushing pink at the base; smells slightly of aniseed.

Cultivated Mushroom, *Agaricus bisporus.* Occasional in fields and gardens and manure. Cap white, browning slightly on the top, 5–10cm (2–4in). Flesh grows slightly pink with age and reddens when cut. Large ring.

DESCRIPTION
Brownish fungus,
5–25cm (2–10cm), with
a short, bulging, pale
brown stem streaked
with white. White, firm,
pleasant-smelling flesh.

CAP
smaller than the stem at
first, older caps brown,
dry and smooth, 8–30cm
(3–12in) across.

GILLS
white at first, then yellow
to olive-brown.

RING
none.

HABITAT
quite common in rides
and clearings in all sorts
of woods, especially
beech,
August–November.

Cep
Boletus edulis

All members of the *Boletus* family are distinguishable by their 'gills', which are in fact a spongy mass of fine tubes or pores beneath the cap. The cep has the additional distinction of looking exactly like a glossy penny bun, to which it is always compared.

Ceps are one of the most famous of all edible fungi and at one time there were six different varieties for sale at Covent Garden. Unfortunately they are equally well-liked by insects, so it is as well to cut the caps in half before cooking to check that they are not infested. To prepare for cooking remove the stem, and scoop away the pores with a spoon (unless they are very young and firm).

As well as being delicious sliced and eaten raw, there are a prodigious number of recipes for ceps. They can be sliced and fried in oil for ten minutes with a little garlic and parsley. They can be fried with potatoes, or grilled with fish. They are excellent for drying (and indeed in the dried form are quite widely available in delicatessens in this country), and reconstitute well after being soaked in warm water. Dried ceps can also be ground into powder and used as flavouring.

One of the most attractive is an old Polish recipe for beetroot and cep soup, which is traditionally served on Christmas Eve. Make some clear beetroot stock by boiling chopped raw beetroots in water, with bay leaves and peppercorns. Take your sliced ceps and fry in butter with chopped onion and paprika pepper for about five minutes. Take some ravioli-shaped pastry cases and fill with the cep and onion mixture, finely minced. Seal the cases, and bake in the oven until golden-brown. Reheat the beetroot stock, and sharpen to taste with a little vinegar and lemon juice. At the last minute add the hot cases and serve.

Most *Boletus* species are mild and nutty to taste, and they are amongst the most popular edible fungi in mainland Europe. There are a large number of boletes growing in the British Isles, and all of them have the same foam-like gill structure. A few are indigestible or can cause bad gastric upsets, but luckily all of these species are coloured red or purple on the pores or stem, and so are easy to identify and therefore to avoid (see devil's bolete, p.163).

Bay Bolete
Xerocomus badius

CAP
similar to *Boletus edulis*, shiny, chestnut to chocolate brown, 7–15cm (3–6in); felt-like when dry, but slightly clammy when wet. Pores pale yellow to yellow-green. Stem yellow-brown, stout but not bulbous. Flesh white to pale yellow; stains blue when cut.

HABITAT
quite common in woodland on acid soils, favours Scots pine. August–November.

Yellow-cracked Bolete
Boletus subtomentosus

CAP
colour is variable, olive-yellow to brown, 5–7cm (2–3in); when old the surface is often cracked. Pores bright yellow. Stem yellow-brown, ribbed, tapering towards the base. Flesh soft, yellowish-white, pleasant smelling. Edible but soft.

HABITAT
found in all sorts of wood, especially in moss and on grassy paths. June–October.

Red-cracked Bolete
Boletus chrysenteron

CAP
colour is variable, usually yellow-brown with a pink layer beneath. Pores yellow to olive, bruising blue. Stem yellow with a reddish tinge. Edible but soggy and can be prone to infestation by maggots.

HABITAT
a common woodland species.

Boletus aerus

CAP
dark brown. Pores and flesh white, bruising wine-coloured. Stem covered with a network of brown veins.

HABITAT
Found with beech and oak.

Gyroporus cyanescens

CAP
yellowish-white in colour, dry and sometimes cracked, 4–10cm (1½–4in). Pores white to pale yellow. Stem stout, velvety, pale ochre. White flesh turns deep blue immediately after cutting.

HABITAT
rare in woods on poor soil, especially spruce. July–December.

Slippery Jack
Suillus luteus

CAP
medium-sized, slimy brown cap 6–12cm (2–5in). Pores white to pale yellow. Stem yellow, with a floppy, brownish-purple ring. Flesh yellow, unchanging when cut. Peel before cooking. Will not keep and therefore unsuitable for drying.

HABITAT
Quite common amongst grass in conifer woods. September–November.

Suillus granulatus

CAP
slimy, straw-yellow to leather-brown cap, 5–8cm (2–3in). peels easily. Pores yellow to olive, and when young exudes milky drops. Stem slender, light yellow, granular, no ring. Flesh yellowish, unchanging when cut; fruity smell. Very susceptible to maggots.

HABITAT
quite common in conifer woods. June–October.

Larch Bolete
Suillus grevillii

CAP

slimy, pale yellow 4–12cm (1½–5in). Pores sulphur yellow, bruise brown. Stem tall, yellow-brown; pale ring soon disappears. Flesh has the colour and texture of rhubarb and stains pale lilac on cutting. Remove skin and tubes before cooking.

HABITAT

quite common in larch woods only. June–November.

Boletus erythropus

CAP

large convex, less than 20 cm (8in) across, chestnut to liver brown in colour. Pores, small, round, deep orange-red; blue when bruised. Stem thick and yellow, covered with red spotting. Flesh yellowish, turning intense blue when cut or broken. Little smell or taste.

HABITAT

common in woodland clearings on acid soils.

Commonly confused with *Boletus satanus* (see below) so best avoided even though it is edible. Other edible species that can be confused with *B. satanus* are: *B. luridus*, *B. queletii* and *B. rhodopurpureus*.

Devil's Bolete
Boletus satanas

CAP

large, soft, almost hemispherical and entirely white, turning greyish with age, 8–25cm (3–10in). Pores tiny, first yellow then red; bruise blue-green. Stem swollen and covered with red veining. Flesh thick and yellow, stains blue when cut; very unpleasant smell.

HABITAT

rare and local in late summer under broad-leaved trees, especially beech and oak, in the south of England.

Poisonous. Very indigestible, and can cause severe gastric complaints in some people.

The *Russula* species

There are over 100 species of *Russula* in Britain. With their brightly coloured caps they are among the most attractive of our native fungi and many (with some notable exceptions, see below) are good to eat. Often specific to a particular species of tree, Russulas are characterised by crumbly flesh.

The Russulas are a difficult family, multi-specied, enormously variable in colouring and yet too good to omit altogether. Their variability can lead almost any specimen, at some stage in its development, to become one of those vague white-gilled, yellowish, greenish or brownish capped fungi which are so difficult to tell from the main poisonous species. None of the Russulas themselves are poisonous when cooked, but there are three common species that are poisonous when raw; these are described below right.

Bare-toothed Russula

Russula vesca

CAP
colour variable, from pale pink to violet or rusty red, 5–10cm (2–4in). Gills: white. Brightly-coloured fungus with a toothed edge to the cap when mature; pure white stem with no ring or sheath.

HABITAT
all types of woodland, especially oak and beech, June–November.

Common Yellow Russula

Russula ochroleuca

CAP
(see photograph above left) ochre-yellow. Stem white, flushed with yellow, becomes greyer with age. Gills cream.

HABITAT
very common in coniferous woods.

Yellow Swamp Russula

Russula claroflava

CAP
matt yellow at first, becoming shiny 5–12cm (2–5in). Gills ochre, stem white, bruising greyish. Flesh is white with a fruity smell and a mild taste

HABITAT
common under birch and alder. June–November.

Green-cracking Russula

Russula virescens

CAP
cream, turns patchy green with age, 4–9cm (1½–4in); central depression. Gills creamy white. This is an excellent fungus, regarded as the best edible Russula, with a mildly nutty taste which has been likened to new potatoes. Do watch out for maggots.

HABITAT
occasional in open woodland, especially oak and beech. May–October.

Russula xerampelina

CAP
blackish-purple in the centre fading to carmine at edge, 8–15cm (3–6 in), with no depression,. Gills ochre, flesh yellowing when cut. Stem has a pink tinge and bruises brown. Smells and tastes of shellfish.

HABITAT
common under pines.

Russula krombholzii

CAP
previously known as R. atropurpurea. A striking deep purple in colour, with a darker centre, 3–10cm (1–4in). Gills, stipe and flesh dull white, smelling slightly of apples.

HABITAT
common throughout Britain, especially under oak. June–December

The Charcoal Burner
Russula cyanoxantha

CAP
a mixture of colours ranging from greenish-blue to violet, 5–15cm (2–6in). Soft, white, elastic gills. Stem and flesh white and firm with little or no smell.

HABITAT
found in broad-leaved woodland, especially with beech.

Russula aeruginea

CAP
greenish-grey, 8–12 cm (3–5in), with no central depression. Gills forked and yellowish. Stipe white, yellowing slightly with age.

HABITAT
quite common under birch and conifers.

The Sickener
Russula emetica

CAP
shiny bright cherry-red or vermilion 5–10cm (2–4in). Gills creamy-white. Stem spongy with a swollen base. Fruity smell.

HABITAT
common under pine or birch.

Beechwood Sickener
Russula mairei

CAP
matt, bright cherry-red or vermilion (3–7cm, 1–3in), pink flesh beneath the skin. Gills white with a grey-green tint. Stem white yellowing at the base. Smells of coconut.

HABITAT
grows under beech.

Both R. emetica and R. mairei are poisonous when raw and best avoided altogether. R aeruginea can cause stomach upsets and should also be avoided.

Leccinum spp.

Brown Birch Bolete
Leccinum scabrum

DESCRIPTION
Medium-sized brown fungus, 8–15cm (3–6in). Stem tall, white, flecked with brown to black scales. Soft flesh soon becomes moist and spongy.

CAP
smooth and greyish-brown; usually dry, but sticky in wet weather, 5–10cm (2–4in). Pores white to dirty brown.

HABITAT
common in grass under birches, July–November.

Although common in birch woodland, only really young caps are worth eating. Make sure they are firm and maggot-free and discard any tubes which can be easily removed. Good for adding to soups and stews.

Orange Birch Bolete
Leccinum versipelle

DESCRIPTION
Large orange-capped fungus 15–25cm (6–10in), with white flesh that slowly turns dirty pink on cutting. Stem sturdy and tapering towards the cap, slate-coloured, scurfy.

CAP
orange-yellow to yellow-brown, 15–25cm (6–10in). Pores minute, dirty grey.

HABITAT
common under birches and conifers, July–November.

Although not as flavorsome as the cep, the flesh of this mushroom is much firmer, and finding one is definitely worthwhile. The cap has a felty texture and is orange-buff in colour with an over-hanging margin. Don't be alarmed by the fact that the flesh turns dark-grey on cooking, this will just confirm your identification!

DESCRIPTION
Large, pale orange, funnel shaped, 3–9cm (1–3½in). Short orange stem.

CAP
5–15cm (2–6in), with bands of deep orange spots, depression in the centre.

GILLS
bright orange, crowded. Produces orange milk when scratched which turns green; older specimens will also be stained green.

HABITAT
with pine trees, September–November.

Please note that this species can be confused with two poisonous relatives:

Lactarius helvus
Also found with pine, this species is distinguished by a lack of bands on the yellow-brown cap, with stem and gills the same colour, and a water-like milk. Smells of fenugreek.

Woolly Milk Cap,
Lactarius torminosus
Found with birch, the stem, gills and cap are flesh-pink. The cap does feature darker rings, but the cap has a woolly appearance, and the milk is white.

Saffron Milk Cap
Lactarius deliciosus

The best of the edible milk caps, the characteristic shape and colour of the saffron milk cap can be seen in a Roman fresco, and the Latin name certainly gives an indication of its culinary value at that time.

Popular in parts of Europe, this fungus has a rich, mild but sometimes bitter flesh. The bitterness can be removed by blanching. Once dried the mushroom can be fried or grilled – the latter is recommended as it makes the most of the crisp texture. It goes well with fish, and its eye-catching colour makes it an attractive addition to any dish.

Another *Lactarius* species, *L. sanguifluus*, is regarded as an excellent edible fungus. It has a reddish-orange cap 4–12cm (2–5in) across, with pinkish zones, and pink gills which become spotted with green when damaged. The flesh is red and exudes a red milk which turns brown. It occurs with pine and is common in southern Europe, but is rarer in the north.

Giant Puffball

Langermannia gigantea

DESCRIPTION
Large and roughly spherical, (usually) 10–30cm (4–12in) across. Skin, white, smooth and leathery initially. Flesh also white, turning to yellow and dirty green when old. Grows apparently straight from the ground with little or no stalk.

HABITAT
Meadows, pastures, sometimes under hedges.
July–November

Giant puffballs are one of the tastiest and most rewarding of all wild foods. To come upon one unexpectedly is always an exciting experience, only rivalled by the taste of the first mouthful. There is not much point in searching deliberately for them. They are almost always unexpected, glinting like displaced, outsized eggs under hedges or in the corners of fields, occasionally growing in groups or fairy rings. When I first began finding them in East Anglia, I can remember wheeling them home supported on my bicycle saddle, for the regular ritual of weighing and measuring. I am still occasionally sent pictures of prize balls posed on bars or sideboards alongside their finders, as if they were a kind of trophy or vegetable pet.

Giant puffballs can grow to impressive sizes and suggestive shapes, and books are full of record specimens and stories of mistaken identity. Workmen in the 1920s found several specimens under a floor at Kew, and mistook them for human skulls. The police were called, but it took the advice of experts at the nearby Royal Botanic Garden to solve the mystery. During the second World War one specimen discovered under an Oak tree in Kent was believed to be a new kind of German bomb. One in New York State was over 1.2m (4ft) in diameter, and was mistaken at a distance for a sheep.

More usually they are the size of a child's football, but even this will provide a meal for a large number of people, since every part of the fungus is solid, edible flesh. The important quality to look out for is that this flesh is still pure white. As it ages, puffball flesh turns yellow and then pale brown, and during these stages the balls become progressively less appetising and increasingly indigestible.

The final mass of greenish-brown dust consists of reproductive spores. The giant puffball is one of the most fecund of all living organisms, and a single specimen may produce up to seven billion spores. When fully ripe they are expelled as a kind of smoke from a hole on top of the dried-out ball: hence the now sadly defunct names 'Puckfist', 'Puffes Fist' or 'Fist Balls' – 'fist' being a polite alternative to 'fart'. Gerard wrote that they are called:

Other puffball species

There are several species of small puffball that are also edible, though they tend to be rubbery in texture and lack the exquisite taste of the giant species. The three commonest are *Vascellum pratense*, which occurs on lawns, short pastures, heaths and golf courses from summer to late autumn, and *Lycoperdon perlatum* and *L. pyriforme*, which are both woodland species often occurring in clusters. All three grow roughly to the size of four golf balls, and are covered by slightly warty white skins. They are edible when young, before the flesh has started to yellow. Cut in slices before frying in bacon fat (as for giant puffball) or, if very young, use sparingly in salads.

'*in English Fusse Ball, Pucke Fuse and Bulfists, with which in some places in England they use to kill and smoulder their Bees, when they would drive the Hives, and bereave the poore Bees of their meate, hose and lives; there are also used in some places where neighbours dwell farre a sunder, to carrie and reserve fire from place to place.*'

A few beekeepers still use whole, dried balls as natural aerosols, to puff spores around the hive when they wish to calm the bees. But the spores are inflammable, and the same effect was sometimes achieved by using the smoke produced by burning dried balls. Similarly, to produce lightning on stage before the days of electrical special effects, a mass of spore dust (often mixed with spores from clubmoss) was ignited and thrown across the area where the effect was required. Puffball dust was also valued as a styptic for small cuts, and – there was doubtless sympathetic magic behind this – for burns. Dried balls were a frequent item once in blacksmiths' shops in East Anglia.

BELOW
Lycoperdon perlatum

Cleaning, preparing, storing

When using puffballs in the kitchen, there is no real need for elaborate preparation or peeling. Simply clean them, and slice then into 1cm (½in) steaks. They can then be fried, grilled or baked, in butter, oil or bacon fat. The slices taken from the smoother, more rubbery flesh near the top of the fungus are like sweetbreads; the more crumbly steaks from near the base are softer and less succulent, a little like an omelette or toasted marshmallow.

Even with small specimens you are likely to be left with some surplus steaks, and collectors have experimented with deep-freezing these. The slices can be frozen fresh, but tend to become rather soggy on thawing. Better results are obtained by coating them in an egg and breadcrumb mixture (see right), frying and them deep-freezing. Perhaps the answer is not to pick the whole puffball at once, but follow the 'cut-and-come-again' practice recommended by Victorian writers who had seen the Italian way with giant puffballs:

'We have known specimens to grow amongst cabbages in a kitchen garden, and when such is the case it may be left standing, slices being cut off as required until the whole is consumed.'

Fried puffball steaks

1 medium-sized puffball

8 rashers of bacon (optional)

Butter or vegetable oil

1 cupful of breadcrumbs

1 egg

50g (2oz) seasoned flour

1 Wipe the puffball clean, and cut into slices about half an inch thick, checking that they are clear of any yellowish tinge. There is no need to peel the ball.

2 Make a batter by beating the flour and egg together until smooth, then slowly adding water until the mixture is the consistency of single cream.

3 Dip each side of the puffball steak into the batter, then into the breadcrumbs (spread them in a shallow dish or on paper for convenience). Toasting the breadcrumbs beforehand makes a crunchy alternative.

4 Leave the battered, crumbed steaks to drain for a few minutes while you fry the bacon.

5 Remove the bacon from the pan, and fry the puffball slices in the fat; butter or vegetable oil can be used instead.

6 Serve with the bacon if using.

DESCRIPTION
An ear-shaped bracket
fungus, 2–7cm (1–3in) in
diameter. Usually grows
in clusters. Red-brown in
colour, and gelatinous
and soft when young.
Upper surface more
velvety and brown,
underside pink.

HABITAT
quite common on elder.
Found throughout the
year, especially October
and November

Jew's Ear

Auricularia auricularia-judae

I can imaging no food more forbidding in appearance than the Jew's ear.
It hangs in folds from decaying elder branches like slices of some ageing
kidney, clammy and jelly-like to the touch. It is no fungus to leave around
the house if you have sensitive relations, or even to forget about in your
own pocket.

But it is a good edible species for all that, and is much prized in China,
where a related species is grown for food on oak palings. It was also valued
by the old herbalists as 'fungus sambuci', a poultice for inflamed eyes,
though apparently not sufficiently to warrant a more complimentary name.
Anti-semitism in the Middle Ages meant that all fungi was known as 'Jew's
meat', though the name may contain an oblique reference to Judas, who
reputedly hanged himself from an elder tree, the host species for *Auricula
auricula-judae*.

Jew's ear should be gathered young while it is still soft and moist (it turns rock hard with age), and cut from the tree with a knife; make sure you discard all of the tough stalk. It should be washed well, and sliced finely, for although the translucent flesh is thin it can be tough and indigestible. Stew for a good three-quarters of an hour in stock or milk, and serve with plenty of pepper. Make sure it is cooked properly otherwise the flesh will be very rubbery. The result is crisp and not unlike a seaweed. It can be dried, and is best ground to a powder and used as a flavouring.

Chinese-style Jew's ear soup

25g (1oz) Jew's ears
800g (2lb) brown sugar crystals
500ml (1 pint) water

1 Clean and soak the fungi and chop roughly.

2 Heat the sugar and water until the sugar melts and the mixture is almost boiling.

3 Drain the Ears, add to the syrup and steam for 1½ hours. Serve hot or cold.

WINTER

'Tis a dull sight

To see the year dying,

When winter winds

Set the yellow wood sighing

OLD SONG, Edward Fitzgerald 1809–1883

DESCRIPTION
An undistinguished
spreading, branched
annual with stiff, upright
stems, 20–150cm
(8–60in).

LEAVES
diamond-shaped, greyish-
green.

FLOWERS
pale green, minute and
bunched into spikes,
June–October.

FRUIT
tiny, each containing one
brown-black seed.

HABITAT
common in cultivated
and waste ground
throughout British Isles.

Fat-hen
Chenopodium album

The ability of this species to thrive anywhere humans settle means that it
is no surprise to find that its use as a food plant dates back to prehistoric
times, and its fatty seeds and abundant leaves must have once been a
valuable source of food. Remains of the plants have been found in
Neolithic settlements all over Europe. The seeds also formed part of the
last, possibly ritual meal fed to Tollund Man, whose perfectly preserved
corpse, including the contents of his stomach, was recovered from a bog
in Jutland, Denmark in 1950. Fat-hen is one of the very first plants to
colonise ground that has been disturbed by roadworks or housebuilding,
its stiff, mealy spikes often appearing in prodigious quantity.

In Anglo-Saxon times the plant was apparently of sufficient
importance to have villages named after it. As 'melde' it is though to have

given its name to Melbourn in
Cambridgeshire, and Milden in
Suffolk. The introduction of
spinach, a domesticated relative,
largely put an end to the use of the
plant as a wild food, but its leaves
continued to be eaten in Ireland
and the Scottish islands for a long
while. We now know that early
people were lucky in this
fortuitous choice of a staple
vegetable: it contains more iron
and protein than either cabbage or
spinach, and more Vitamin B1
and calcium than raw cabbage.

The whole plant can be eaten
raw, but is probably best prepared
and cooked in the same way as
spinach, as a green vegetable, or in
soups. It is pleasantly tangy, like
young kale or broccoli.

Wild Cabbage

Brassica oleracea

DESCRIPTION
Hairless perennial with thick stems and a woody base, up to 1.5m (5ft).

LEAVES
greyish. lower leaves large, lobed; upper leaves unlobed partly clasping the stem.

FLOWERS
yellow, in long clusters, May–September.

HABITAT
sea cliffs and rocks, on dry stony soils.

This scarce plant of the sea cliffs in parts of Wales and southern England, is a variety of the same species as our cultivated cabbages, but whether it is the ancestor of these cultivated varieties, or whether the wild species originated from cultivated forms in ancient settlements, is a difficult question to answer.

They have thick, greyish, fleshy leaves. They are bitter raw, but after long simmering are acceptable to eat.

RIGHT
Wild cabbage, Foreland Point, Dorset

Shepherd's Purse

Capsella bursa-pastoris

DESCRIPTION
A downy, branched annual, 5–60cm (2–24in).

LEAVES
spear-shaped and deeply lobed, in a neat basal rosette.

FLOWERS
small with white petals and pink calyx; can flower all year in mild conditions.

FRUIT
in small, heart-shaped pods, like purses.

HABITAT
abundant and widespread in waste and cultivated places.

Common in waste places throughout the British Isles, shepherd's purse is one of the first wild plants to flower, and will sometimes flower all through mild winters. It has a slightly peppery taste, and is popular in China, where it is stir-fried, like cabbage and Chinese leaf.

Watercress
Rorippa nasturtuim-aquaticum

DESCRIPTION
Aquatic hairless
perennial, creeping or
floating, 10–50cm
(4–20in).

LEAVES
rich, silky green leaflets,
slightly toothed.

FLOWERS
a bunch of small white
blossoms, May–October.

HABITAT
grows abundantly in and
by running water
throughout the British
Isles.

Most of the watercress we eat today is grown commercially; but the cultivated plants are identical in every respect to those that grow wild, sometimes in great green hillocks, on the muddy edges of all freshwater streams. Traditionally picked wild from fast-flowing streams, watercress was certainly under small-scale cultivation by the middle of the 18th Century, and quickly became a commercial product as the fast-growing science of nutrition caught a glimpse of its anti-scorbutic properties (which result, as we know now, from an exceptionally high Vitamin C content).

The plants to pick are not the young ones, which are rather tasteless, but the older, sturdier specimens, whose darker leaves have a slight burnish to them. These are the tangy ones, which justify the plant's Latin name, *Nasi-tortium*, meaning 'nose-twisting'. Never pick watercress from stagnant water, or slow-moving streams, which flow through pastureland. Watercress can be a host to one stage in the life cycle of the fluke, *Fasciola hepatica*, which can cause liver damage in sheep and cattle, and will also attack humans. Although boiling kills the larvae, it is best to avoid picking specimens that are likely to be infested. Do this by choosing beds growing in fast-flowing, clean water, not adjacent to the riverbank – although this will involve good balance and a sturdy pair of wellingtons. Do not pull up the plants by the root, cut the tops of the shoots and wash well wherever they have been growing.

Wild watercress makes a good cooked vegetable, especially if spiked with orange and lemon juice and chopped hazelnuts. Watercress soup can be made by boiling two bunches of watercress, roughly chopped, in stock made from two large potatoes, a pint of water and seasoning. Cook for ten minutes, put through a liquidiser, add a little cream if desired, and serve chilled.

Alexanders
Smyrnium olustratum

DESCRIPTION
A bushy, solid-stemmed hairless biennial, to 1.2m (4ft).

LEAVES
glossy, toothed, on groups of three at the end of leaf stalk; the other end being joined to the main stem by a substantial sheath.

FLOWERS
umbels of yellow-green flowers, April–June.

HABITAT
widespread and locally abundant in hedgebanks and waste places, especially near the sea.

The Romans brought alexanders to this country from the Mediterranean as a pot-herb – the 'parsley of Alexandria'. It thrived, became naturalised, and was still being planted in kitchen gardens in the early 18th Century.

The most succulent part of the plant is the stem. You should cut those leaf stems which grow near the base of the plant, where they are thick and have been partially blanched by the surrounding grass or the plant's own foliage. Cook the stems in boiling water for not more than ten minutes, then eat them like asparagus, with melted butter. They have a delicate texture, and a pleasantly aromatic taste.

Goosegrass, Cleavers
Galium aparine

DESCRIPTION
A straggling, bristly annual 50–180cm (20–70in) with square stems.

LEAVES
narrow, pointed, in whorls of 6–8 leaves, covered with tiny turned-down prickles.

FLOWERS
inconspicuous, white, greenish-white, May–June.

HABITAT
widespread and abundant in hedges, woods and cultivated ground.

Rest assured that after this plant has been plunged into boiling water for a few seconds, the hook-like bristles covering goosegrass lose their sharpness. Briefly boiled or steamed as a green vegetable before the hard round seeds appear, goosegrass makes tolerable if stringy eating, and can usually be gathered in sufficient quantities to make an ample dishful. Moreover, it can be picked through the snow and frost when few other green plants are to be found. John Evelyn recommended the young shoots in spring soups and puddings.

Dead-nettles

The young shoots and leaves of these common and familiar weeds can be washed and cooked with no additional water but with a knob of butter, salt and pepper and some chopped spring onions, for about ten minutes. Finish with a dash of lemon juice or a sprinkling of nutmeg.

White dead-nettle
Lamium album

DESCRIPTION
A hairy, patch-forming perennial with a square stem, to 60cm (24in).

LEAVES
in pairs, triangular, pointed and coarsely toothed.

FLOWERS
creamy-white in whorls, March–November.

HABITAT
widespread and common on roadsides, in hedgebanks, waste places and gardens; rare and local in the north and west of Scotland and south-west Ireland.

Red dead-nettle
Lamium purpureum

DESCRIPTION
Downy, often purple-tinged annual, 10–40cm (4–16in).

LEAVES
in pairs, heart-shaped, toothed and pointed.

FLOWERS
pinkish-purple in whorls; can flower all year in mild conditions.

HABITAT
widespread and abundant in cultivated ground.

Henbit dead-nettle
Lamium amplexicaule

DESCRIPTION
Hairy annual, to 30cm (12in), with a square green or reddish stem.

LEAVES
rounded, bluntly-toothed, top leafs partly clasping the stem.

FLOWERS
pinkish-purple in whorls; March–October.

HABITAT
widespread and abundant in cultivated and waste ground.

DESCRIPTION
Slender annual, 5–20cm
(2–8in).

LEAVES
oblong, slightly toothed,
in pairs.

FLOWERS
tiny lilac, flat-topped
clusters, April–August.

HABITAT
quite common in arable
ground, on banks and
walls.

Cornsalad, Lamb's Lettuce
Valerianella locusta

A small plant with oval leaves that have a succulent texture but little flavour. It is however, a useful addition to salads, especially as it stays in leaf for most of the winter. Lamb's lettuce and its cultivated relatives are popular in France, where they are known as *mache* and *salade de prêtre*. Now widely cultivated, the leaves are best served with a sharp dressing to bring out their flavour and texture.

DESCRIPTION
A sturdy, ferny perennial
growing in clumps and
patches, 10–100cm
(4–40in), strong-
smelling.

LEAVES
dark-green, feathery.

FLOWERS
creamy-white disc florets
and pink ray florets in
flat-topped clusters;
sometimes flowers until
Christmas.

HABITAT
grows in abundance in
grassy places.

Yarrow
Achillea millefolium

The Anglo-Saxons regarded yarrow as a powerful herb, providing protection against bad luck and illness. It also had a great reputation amongst herbalists as an astringent for wounds, although it was also believed to cause nosebleeds if one of the feathery leaves (the Latin name *millefolium* means 'thousand-leaf') went up the nose.

Used in small quantities it can make a cool if rather bitter addition to salads.

Milk Thistle

Silybum marianum

DESCRIPTION
Spiny annual-biennial, to 1.5m (5ft) with downy stems.

LEAVES
dark green, spiny, with intricate white veins.

FLOWERS
purple, June–August; bracts end in yellow spines.

HABITAT
widespread but locally common in waste places the British Isles; favours areas near the sea, and especially the Thames estuary

This handsome thistle was introduced into western European gardens from the Mediterranean before the 16th Century, for use as a medicinal herb. The spiny, white-veined leaves were believed to increase the milk output of nursing mothers.

Almost all parts of the plant were eaten. Bryant, in his *Flora Dietetica*, writes of it: 'The young shoots in the spring, cut close to the root with part of the stalk on, is one of the best boiling salads that is eaten, and surpasses the finest cabbage. They were sometimes baked in pies. The roots may be eaten like those of Salsify.' The leaves were trimmed of prickles and boiled. The stems were peeled, soaked in water to remove the bitterness, and then stewed like rhubarb. Even the spiny bracts that surround the broad flower-head were eaten like globe artichokes.

Dandelion

Taraxacum officinale

DESCRIPTION

tufty, hairy perennial, 5–40cm (2–16in), with hollow stems; the whole plant exudes a milky juice when cut.

LEAVES

roughly toothed, growing from the base of the plant.

FLOWERS

large, golden-yellow, comprising numerous fine petals; February–November, but especially April and May.

HABITAT

widespread and abundant in open and grassy places throughout British Isles.

The dandelion is one of the most profuse of British weeds, and in late spring is liable to cover almost any grassy place with its blazing yellow flowers. Its leaves – and consequently its roots – can be found at almost any time of the year except the very coldest, which is welcome, given the wide range of food uses to which the plant can be put.

The Japanese use the root as a vegetable. Chop the scrubbed roots into thin rings. Sauté these in vegetable oil, using about one tablespoonful of oil to one cup of chopped roots. Then add a small amount of water, a little salt, and cover the pan. Stew until the roots are soft and most of the moisture and added water have evaporated. Finally add a dash of soy sauce.

It is especially useful as a salad plant, since the leaves can be gathered at almost any time of the year. Only after prolonged frost or snow is it

impossible to find any. Choose the youngest leaves and strip them from the plant by hand. (If you have dandelions growing in your garden, try manuring them and covering the lower parts of the leaves with earth or a cardboard tube to blanch them like chicory. They did this in medieval gardens and produced gigantic plants as a result.) When you have sufficient leaves, trim off any excess stalk, and wash well. The roughly chopped leaves can be made into a good salad simply by dressing with olive oil, lemon juice and a trace of garlic. They can also be served in sandwiches with a dash of Worcester sauce, or cooked with butter like spinach.

Truffle
Tuber aestivum

DESCRIPTION
An underground fungus, about the size of a golf ball, 3–7cm (1–3in), with a strong, pleasant smell.

FRUITBODY
outside has a warty appearance; blue-black when fresh, turning to brown-black. Flesh yellow-white, later brown with white marbling.

HABITAT
rare, sometimes found in woodland in south of England, prefers limestone soils.

The highly-prized Perigord or black truffle (*Tuber melanosporum*) is not found in this country. The summer truffle, *T. aestivum*, is not uncommon, but is not easy to find. It is an underground fungus and, like other truffles, is all but impossible to find without a specially-trained animal. Indeed it is the animals themselves that help disperse the spores which are stored inside the fruitbody.

Truffle-hunting is still part of rural economies in mainland Europe, particularly in France and Italy, and there was once a lively traffic in them in some of the southern counties of England, where they were sniffed out of beech woods by Spanish poodles. The last professional truffle hunter in Britain, Alfred Collins, retired in 1930. Before that time truffle hunting in the Winterslow area of Wiltshire had a tradition going back 300 years. Between November and March Alfred would scour the countryside together with his dogs. Dogs have to be trained to dig out truffles, in the same way that they are trained to sniff out drugs by police and customs officers, but pigs do not have to be trained and will hunt for truffles naturally. Apparently Alfred Collins became so experienced in his trade that he could smell the truffles while they were still in the ground (the dogs were able to smell them from 20m away), he could also feel them underfoot and judge from clouds of flies whether a truffle was lying beneath the topsoil.

It was clearly a thriving small business, providing income for all sorts of people. In a 1971 article for *Country Life*, J. E. Manners described how the fungi were distributed:

> '*Truffles were invariably sold to private customers so they rarely came on the market. They only kept for about four days before losing flavour so they were always posted off as soon as possible in cardboard shoe boxes, which the children collected from the bootmaker for a penny each. They could be preserved in vinegar.*'

Although the milder flavour of the summer truffle is inferior to that of its Perigord counterpart, it should certainly be regarded as an exciting find.

Gently brush any soil away from the skin and make sure you slice it thinly to get maximum use out of it! It can be added to stuffings and pâtés, and can make luxurious omelettes or scrambled eggs. Rose Elliot creates a sumptuous soufflé omelette using shavings of precious truffle. This cross between an omelette and a soufflé is created by folding beaten egg whites

ABOVE
False truffle, *Elaphomyces granulatus.*

into egg yolks that have been mixed well with a little water and seasoning. This mixed is then poured into a heated and buttered pan and cooked until golden underneath. Then put the pan under the grill until the top of the omelette is golden. Make a cut across the middle of the omelette (but not right through), sprinkle the truffle shavings over one half, fold the other half over and then serve with a little flat-leaf parsley sprinkled over the top. The truffle can also be used to flavour oil, which also serves to preserve the fungus, but it will reduce the flavour. Truffle oil is very rich and should be used sparingly.

T. aestivum can be confused with the false truffle, *Elaphomyces granulatus*. This is one of the most frequently-found underground fungi as it frequently appears with the parasitic club-shaped fungus *Cordyceps ophioglossoides* which emerges above the ground. It develops just below the surface in woodland soil, especially in coniferous woods with pine. About the size of a large marble – the ones that used to be so highly prized at school – the false truffle's firm skin is thick, warty and red-brown. The flesh is flexked purple-brown and darkens as the spores mature. This species is not edible and when uncovered can be told by the fact it has no distinctive smell.

Oyster Mushroom
Pleurotus ostreatus

DESCRIPTION
A fan-shaped bracket fungus, found growing on tree trunks or branches in shelves up to 20cm (8in) across.

CAP
well-shaped, convex at first, then flat, grey or slate-blue in colour.

GILLS
white and deep. Flesh white, soft, rubbery.

HABITAT
found on dead or dying branches of beech and ash; common round the year, though principally in late autumn and winter.

The oyster mushroom tends to be rather tough, and you should choose young specimens and cook them thoroughly. Inspect carefully for maggots when cleaning. Try slicing into pieces not more than 1cm (½in) thick, sprinkling with a few drops of lemon juice, turning in seasoned flour, then in beaten egg and finally in breadcrumbs. The slices should then be fried in deep oil until golden. They can also be grilled, added to stew and casseroles, and dried.

Because of their comparatively mild flavour, oyster mushrooms can be served with fairly rich sauces. Try slicing them about 1cm (½in) thick, and frying in oil for five minutes until their juices begin to flow. Sprinkle a little flour into the pan, and then stir in a glass of Madeira or sherry. Add a beaten egg yolk and seasoning. The simmer and stir until the mixture thickens. Serve on toast or fried bread.

Velvet Shank, Velvet Foot

Flammulina velutipes

DESCRIPTION
Tufts of orange-yellow caps on curved, downy stems, yellow darkening to dark brown, 3–8cm (1–3in)

CAP
small, 2–8cm (1–3in) in diameter, sticky and glistening, honey-yellow to orange-red in colour.

GILLS
broad and tan. Flesh is thin, whitish and rubbery with no smell.

HABITAT
common in clusters on stumps and trunks September–March.

This is one of the few fungi able to survive through frosts. During the winter months there is consequently very little chance that it might be confused with another species.

They can be picked while frozen, and either stored in a deep-freeze or added to stews and casseroles. Make sure you discard the stems and wipe the stickiness off the cap before using them. Add a few towards the last stages of cooking a stew and they will float to the surface like fungal water-lilies.

Sources, References and Further Reading

General and Historical

Austin, Thomas (ed.), *Two Fifteenth Century Cook Books*, Early English Text Society, 1888

Brothwell, Don and Patricia, *Food in Antiquity*, 1969

Burkill, I. H. *Habits of Man and the Origins of Cultivated Plants in the Old World*, Proc. Linn. Soc. 164, 1953

Candolle, A de, *Origines des Plantes Cultiveès*, Paris 1883

Culpeper, Nicholas, *The Complete Herbal*, 1653

Drummond, C., and Wilbraham, Anne, *The Englishman's Food*, 1957

Evelyn, John, *Acetaria: A Discourse of Sallets*, 1699. Facsimile, 1982

Gerard, John, *The Herbal*. Revised and enlarged by Thomas Johnson, 1633 (facsimile edition Dover, New York, 1975)

Giles, W. F., 'Our vegetables, when they came', *Royal Horticultural Society Journal*, Vol. 69, 1944

Godwin, H., *The History of British Flora*, 1956

Greenoak, Francesca, *Forgotten Fruit*, 1983

Grigson, Geoffrey, *The Englishman's Flora*, 1958. Revised ed., 1987

Grigson, Geoffrey, *A Herbal of All Sorts*, 1959

Grigson, Jane, *Jane Grigson's Fruit Book*, 1982

Grigson, Jane, *Jane Grigson's Vegetable Book*, 1978

Hartley, Dorothy, *Food in England*, 1954

Helbaek, H., 'Studying the diet of ancient man,' *Archaeology 14*, 1961

Henslow, G., 'The origin and history of our garden vegetables', *Royal Horticultural Society Journal*, Vol. 36, 37, 1910-11

Hutchins, Sheila, *English Recipes*, 1967

Hyams, Edward, *Plants in the Service of Man*, 1971

Johnson, Charles, *The Useful Plants of Great Britain*, 1862

Lovelock, Yann, *The Vegetable Book*, 1972

Markham, Gervase, *The English Hus-Wife*, 1615

Masefield, G. B., Wallis, M., Harrison, S. G., Nicholson, B. E., *The Oxford Book of Food Plants*, 1969

Mead, W. E., *The English Medieval Feat*, 1931

Ministry of Agriculture, *British Poisonous Plants*, 1954. Revised edition, 1986

North, Pamela, *Poisonous Plants and Fungi*, 1967

Pirie, N. W., *Food Resources: Conventional and Novel*, 1969

Salisbury, Sir Edward, *Weeds and Aliens*, 1961

Sole, William, *Menthae Britannicae*, 1798

Stearn, W. T., 'The origin and later development of cultivated plants' *Royal Horticultural Society Journal*, Vol. 90, 1965

Stevenson, Violet (Ed.), *A Modern Herbal*, 1974

Trease, G. E., *A Textbook of Pharmacognosy*, 1961

Tudge, Colin, *Future Cook*, 1980

Turner, William, *The Herbal*, 1568

Wallis, T. E., *Textbook of Pharmacognosy*, 1960

White, Florence, *Good Things in England*, 1968

Wilson, C. Anne, *Food and Drink in Britain*, 1973

Wild Food Guides

Eley, Geoffrey, *Wild Fruits and Nuts*, 1976

Eley, Geoffrey, *101 Wild Plants for the Kitchen*, 1977

Hatfield, Audrey Wynne, *How to Enjoy Your Weeds*, 1969

Hedrick, U. P. (Ed.), *Sturtevant's Edible Plants of the World* (1919). New edition 1970

Hill, Jason, *The Wild Foods of Britain*, 1939

Jordan, Michael, *A Guide to Wild Plants*, 1976

Loewenfield, Claire, and Black, Philippa, *The Complete Book of Herbs and Spices*, 1974

Loewenfield, Claire, *Nuts*, 1957

Mauduit, Vicomte de, *They Can't Ration These*, 1940

Michael, Pamela, *All Good Things Around Us*, 1980

Ministry of Food, *Hedgerow Harvest*, 1943

Peterson, Vicki, *The Natural Food Catalogue*, 1978

Philipps, Roger, *Wild Food*, 1983

Richardson, Rosamund, *Hedgerow Cookery*, 1980

Ranson, F., *British Herbs*, 1949

Scott, Armoret, *Hedgerow Harvest*, 1979

Urquhart, Judy, *Living off Nature*, 1980

White, Florence, *Flowers as Food*, 1952

Identification Guides

Akeroyd, J., *Collins Wild Guide Wild Flowers*, 1996

Courtecuisse, R. *Collins Wildlife Trust Guide Mushrooms of Britain and Europe*, 1999

Fitter, R., Fitter, A., Blamey, M., *Collins Pocket Guide Wild Flowers of Britain and Europe*, fifth edition 1996

Harding, P., Lyons, T., Tomblin, G., *How to Identify Edible Mushrooms*, 1996

Harding, P., Tomblin, G., *How to Identify Trees*, 1998

Hayward, P., Nelson-Smith, T., Shields, C., *Collins Pocket Guide Sea Shore*, 1996

Heukels, P., *Collins Wildlife Trust Guide Wild Flowers of Britain and Europe*, 2000

Press, B., *Collins Wild Guide Trees*, 1996

Rushforth, K., *Collins Wildlife Trust Guide Trees of Britain and Europe*, 1999

Spooner, B., *Collins Wild Guide Mushrooms and Toadstools*, 1996

Index